Writing for the
Corporate Market
How to Make Big Money
Freelancing for Business

George Sorenson

M L P

MID-LIST PRESS
DENVER

Copyright © 1990 George Sorenson
Published by Mid-List Press, P.O. Box 20292, Denver, CO 80220
First Edition

Library of Congress Cataloging-in-Publication Data

Sorenson, George, 1951-
    Writing for the corporate market: how to make big money
freelancing for business / George Sorenson.
        p.   cm.
    ISBN 0-922811-06-7: $18.95—ISBN 0-922811-07-5 (pbk.):$12.95
    1. Journalism, Commercial. 2. Freelance journalism. 3. Business
report writing. 4. Commercial correspondence. I. Title.
PN4784.C7S67   1990
808' .06607—dc20

Manufactured in the USA

For Wiley Shaver, my 11th-grade English teacher at Crawford High School in San Diego, California. After a career in the army he gave his love of literature to students, brought the language to life, and gifted us with his pure enjoyment of the written word.

For Lynne and Larry Block, with their elucidating insights and support.

For Joey the television director, Bruce the plumber, and Jayme and Cameron the nieces.

CONTENTS

EDITORIAL PREFACE

A survey in a national periodical listed 50 occupations in decreasing order of average income from the highest (professional basketball players) to the very lowest (migrant farm workers and writers). Almost all writers of fiction, nonfiction, and poetry who eat regularly and hope to have enough money to send their children to college require other jobs. Some jobs fit comfortably with their personal writing. Teaching and journalism, for example. Some do not, but have to be endured to sustain life in the face of one's implacable, if not addictive, *need* to write. In this presentation the author suggests a compatible and profitable way to support your writing habit—by writing, of all things. Freelance writing for business. To gain the freedom to write for yourself.

Chapter 1

Getting Into the Writing Cash Flow

Sure You Can Do It!

You probably never envisioned yourself writing marketing or advertising copy. Until now you may have thought of public relations as something a company needs when they have to cover up a mistake. Like changing the flavor of the world's most popular soft drink after spending zillions in bum research, then scrambling to put the best face on the problem when the whole world hollers, "Change it back, you idiots!"

I'd dare to guess you've had it in mind to be a writer for some time, maybe—like me—since you were old enough to hold a big thick lead pencil in your fist in elementary school.

Much as you were fascinated by it, writing was never presented to you as a clear career path. No guidance counselor ever sat you down and recommended you write for a living.

This is not what you heard:

"Freelance writing will help you be all you can be."

"It's a cozy and comfortable profession."

"Good prospects in the writing trade, with great security and a fine future for most people."

The prospects were too glum or simply unknown to the people giving you advice. So you were steered toward a more solid professional career, like teaching, medicine, or becoming a lawyer.

Truth is, that when you brought up writing as a career, you were told over and over again: "There is no money in writing." "You can't earn a living as a writer." Or, "You know, you're going to have to go out and get a regular job someday, one where you report to work in the morning and get a paycheck every two weeks." My father told me that.

And you've heard this one—"You want to be a writer? What do you have to fall back on?"

Like the rest of us, you never quite gave up the dream of writing for a living. The idea's always been anchored out there, ready for you to figure out a way to hop aboard and set sail.

How can you do it? It seems practically impossible these days to earn a living writing—unless you want to live in a tent and be broke all the time.

Freelance writing for business—corporate communications, marketing and advertising—provides the opportunity you have been looking for. Writing for business is the most realistic way of developing a good steady income from writing today. It is the only type of freelance writing that will allow you to earn enough money to live comfortably and work on "your own" writing.

So, let's imagine you do move into freelance business writing. You research it so you understand your market. Gradually you develop a plan to introduce yourself to clients and go after assignments. Eventually you're going at it full time and full blast.

You enjoy the ruffle and flurry of the advertising world, and find your ability to ride above the hype much better than you thought. In time you have good consistent clients who have interesting products and services.

Your communications skills improve. Your typing speed soars, error rate drops to near zero, and you can actually get the words out faster than you can think of them. The level of confidence you have in your writing is very high and you feel secure in earning a living by writing. Your freelance writing career can continue as long as you'd like.

Some types of projects will be challenging. Some you'll be willing to do for free, as a service to the community. Others you won't do at all because no one could possibly pay you enough to make them worth your while.

A great feature of freelance business writing is it lets you change the texture of your life, as you change what you write about.

If you decide you want to be a private pilot, writing an article on flight instructions may allow you to write off some of the expense of that training. When the travel bug bites, writing a story about a resort area may give you certain privileges where you're staying that other visitors don't have.

And if, in your heart of hearts, you always wanted to write a short story collection or complete a novel, your business writing office can just as effectively be a place where you create literature as it is a place to produce the copy for brochures promoting a business client's products.

Freelancing gives you flexibility in managing your time. If you like to write in the mornings, block out your calendar until noon every day to work on your own writing. Try it for a week and see if you have enough time left in the afternoons to go to business writing meetings and do that work. If not, rearrange your time. Freelancing allows you to change your schedule to satisfy your own writing needs.

This book can help you make a success at writing for business—whether you want to establish a full-time freelance career or just make some extra money writing in your spare time. The information here is also helpful to people who work for businesses and have writing responsibilities. Tips in these chapters on how to handle meetings, get assignments approved, and define responsibilities can make a big difference in the quality of the writing you produce, sell, or just get credit for. This is a practical manual on how to get into the writing cash flow. It is an irreverent guide, inasmuch as it honestly explains the situations you will face and how to deal successfully with them. No punches are pulled. You get a realistic background in this lucrative writing field, along with the framework essential to developing your own effective style of taking on the business writing market. Some people wonder if they want to "waste time" trying to do this type of writing. It seems strange and formal to them. It may seem crassly commercial. They sense an inflexible structure to the writing and see the business world as a foreign environment. Right off, it's important to recognize something about this writing. Writing for business is not an escape from other writing. The difference between business writing and any other writing is mainly the sort of client you have to please. All the writing skills you've developed can be put right to work and they will improve. You have everything to gain as a writer.

What Makes Me So Sure

This is an opinionated guide to freelance writing for marketing, advertising, public relations, technical and general business. Many other books have been written about writing, freelancing, organizing your time, getting your head together, overcoming writer's block, handling your finances, making stationery look good, selling to magazines, and other practical aspects of making a living writing.

You probably should read all of these books if you want to make a living as a writer. You'll need all the help you can get. There is no harder job, certainly none with so little consistent praise or compensation. And there is none that attracts people and then frustrates them so completely—often for their entire lives.

Detailed here is one way to get into the writing cash flow. This is written from the perspective of a successful freelance business writer who never worked for an ad agency or in a company's marketing department. In fact, I've never collected a regular paycheck anywhere, save a five-month stint after college—and that was in a bookstore.

Today my livelihood is completely derived from freelance writing. Not from doing articles for magazines or newspapers. These don't pay enough to earn me a good living. My success comes from freelance writing for business. This same kind of writing can earn you a good living—and put you into a situation where you can be paid to practice your writing every day. Freelance business writing can reward you as no other writing market can.

Your first reaction to the idea of writing for companies may be negative. Perhaps you have the dream of writing fiction. In the past, many great writers have paid their dues and trained themselves by writing nonfiction. Ernest Hemingway supported himself in Paris partly by writing nonfiction articles for newspapers and magazines. Walt Whitman, Theodore Dreiser, and Mark Twain learned the craft of writing through working as journalists.

Times have changed. Today, it is very difficult to earn a living writing for newspapers and magazines, even if you're on their staff. Freelancing for these publications is tough. In fact, magazines are paying less today for freelance articles than they were 50 years ago. And the number of competing writers seems to have increased logarithmically.

Today a full-time entry-level job at a newspaper will require a master's degree in journalism. Magazine staff positions pay poorly, and the competition for them is intense.

In the future, more and more successful writers will be spending time doing business writing. Business communications is the one field where money is available to support writers and let their writing skills blossom. So whoever amounted to anything writing for business?

Kurt Vonnegut wrote for the public relations department of General Electric. The author of *Catch 22*, Joseph Heller, did ad agency work for years, and "wrote" at night. Writers as diverse as E.B. White and suspense writer Lawrence Block did short stints in advertising writing.

Why not just go work for an ad agency?

Ad agencies are often more interested in selling their clients advertising space in magazines and on TV than they are in creating an inventive product. A large percentage of their income comes through ad placement fees. Good writing is less important to them. Money is the overriding issue. This makes it more difficult for a writer to grow in the turmoil of a typical ad agency. The level of hype is very high and the competition—both inside and outside the agency—all consuming.

Freelancing for business is the way out of these traps. By selling your writing ability to companies, both large and small, you can practice your writing while working on personal writing that is important to you—whether it's poetry, novels, short stories, or nonfiction pieces. And freelance business writing can be a writing career in itself, providing you with interesting work and a good income. If you want, there is really no limit to the amount you can make. Practically speaking, you can expect to earn about the same income as your clients. You will find that generally in the range of $20 to $100,000 or more annually.

You can also make a great deal more or less, depending on your willingness to do the things essential to succeed and the amount of time you wish to spend on your personal writing.

My suggestions for the ways to run your freelance business writing career are very specific. All of them are proven. They are the ways I found to make the most money, doing my best writing for the greatest number of clients.

Of course, you have to develop your own style of doing your work and dealing with clients. Adapt my suggestions to an approach you feel comfortable with. When doing this, it is essential that you never exceed your writing skill level or ability to handle a particular type of account, but as you develop your own style and expertise, you'll learn to know your capabilities.

False Images That Inhibit You

One of the greatest hurdles freelance writers have is getting over the idea that business clients, particularly big corporations, are unapproachable monsters. The people who work in these contemporary conglomerates seem, from the outside, to be austere executives, championing the concerns of capitalism, while stiffly dressing in dour pinstripe suits. Nothing could be farther from the truth. As you increase your business contacts, you'll see how fragile the system of business communications really is.

More importantly, you will see how badly businesses need you—the professional with writing skill. Corporations today desperately need people to come in and help them figure out what it is they are trying to say, to whom they're trying to say it, and how to influence those people.

It might not seem easy at first. You'll need to be ready to tough it out, and you'll have to promote your writing in your own way. Forget any stereotyped images of companies and look at each one only as a potential client for your writing. There's a great big writing market out there, ready for you to tap.

No Occupation Is Perfect

While the good aspects usually outweigh the bad, freelance business writing will never be satisfying to you in every way. Some days you will wonder how you ever got the idea to get into it. Nothing about it will make any sense. The personalities you've had to deal with in any one day can make you certain that the state mental hospital is where your client company has been recruiting its employees.

To be blunt, most other types of writing are more satisfying. It is rare that you are able to express yourself in business writing, although opportunities do present themselves from time to time. The advantage of pursuing freelance business writing is the amount of money you can make (and the independence it gives you for personal writing).

Additionally, your client is usually spending a lot of money to make your words look good on paper. The costs of typesetting, designing, and printing the materials are terrifically expensive—so they just plain look nice. It feels good to see what you've written well presented. This allows you to put together a pleasing portfolio, helping build your self confidence, and opening the door to more and larger clients.

The Zero Debt Theory

Because writing is an occupation that takes a good deal of concentration, many writers feel they need to set aside vast amounts of time for their work.

Many people who want to work on their own writing are caught in the bind between time and money. Writers have come up with ingenious ways to give themselves this time. Some have spouses who support them. Others take on low paying, part-time work and dig into their writing on days off.

The worst is the plight of the individual writer who goes after grant money. Grants for writers seldom exceed a few thousand dollars. And to get even that takes mountains of paper work, with samples of your work reviewed by a jury of insiders. Even if you get a grant, by the time you count the hours you've put into the application process, the financial return is microscopic.

What often happens to writers in a financial crunch is something I call the Zero Debt Theory of managing your writing life. It is a theory that wastes more time and talent than any other way of setting up your life as a writer that I know. It is the theory that a writer with a bent for self expression can do better work if not distracted by the worldly matters of having to earn the money to pay rent or buy things. A person subscribing to this tries to build up enough capital to be self-sufficient for an extended time without working. If you have no debt and don't have to worry about money, it will be possible to sit down and let the words flow out. So The Theory supposes.

I have tried this Zero Debt Theory. It does not work. When I have no constraints on my time—nothing to anticipate; no tensions; no healthy level of stress, even if it comes from earning money to pay my bills—my writing goes flat. With no motivational input I have no writing output.

Getting into the mainstream of cash flow is the way to keep involved in what the world's doing and a positive force for getting your writing done.

Freelance business writing helps you to do this. It sharpens your skills and helps you create your own tailored writing environment. It can let you set yourself up with a good typewriter or word processor and put together the resources you need to make your writing work for you.

Freelance business writing can give you confidence that your work is salable. You see your work in print amazingly fast in some cases. When a project is moving along, it can go from your typed draft to four color printing in just hours.

There is great satisfaction in this.

Too, you can get into the minds of many creative people. Working with visual artists, such as graphic designers and illustrators, is very healthy. They have the same conceptual and creative problems you face, only theirs are visual—so it's interesting to see how they handle subjects differently from you.

Although as a writer you may still have the idea that it is best to take yourself out of the flow of everyday life. You may dream of having all the time you want to spend on just writing with no other concerns.

Some writer friends of mine know the grandson of an American family who established a business empire early in this century. The grandson grew up with everything he wanted—cars, boats, travel, and exposure to all the interesting things money can buy. After his education in private schools and passage through a notable Eastern university, he led a relaxed life, trying to put things together for himself just as everyone else does at about that age.

The man is now middle-aged, living in Europe on a trust fund that sends a tidy check his way once a month. The substantial monies are invested and reinvested by a trusted investment firm, so he really has nothing to worry about.

He can do anything he wants, and he wants to be a writer.

Guess what his biggest complaint is? He only wishes he absolutely had to write for his livelihood. Then he would be pushed to write, and it wouldn't have to be something he had to try to make himself do. This man, who never has to worry about making a living, is blocked by not needing to write to survive.

Aren't we lucky to want to write—and to be financially forced to do it at the same time?

Opportunities

If you want to make a living as a writer, there is one market that you can count on. This market offers clients with the best cash flow, who originate the greatest amount of work on a regular basis and are most apt to hire you, regardless of your experience.

This is writing for business. Business writing includes advertising, marketing, and a wide range of other communication materials. It can mean writing individual ads for newspapers or creating a year's worth of slick magazine ads for national magazines. You may have the opportunity to help a real estate developer find people to lease space in a new building with a brochure you've written, or write a booklet for a national sales force that needs guidance from its headquarters' office.

Or any of a thousand other types of writing.

Business writing is where the cash flow is. Companies exist to make a profit, and they need ways to get their messages across. They need good writing to sell a product or service, communicate with their employees or customers, and to handle a million different matters.

Some of the writing opportunities in business involve:

Advertising: From the basics of a local newspaper ad to full blown media campaigns for radio, TV, and national publications.

Marketing: Determining what audience your client needs to address, then finding the best way of communicating your client's message to that audience is the service you offer here.

Public Relations: Press releases are the most obvious writing tasks in PR. Other assignments in this area can be background materials for corporate officers or the writing of articles on most any subject. When you write articles for public relations departments, you can be paid much more for your writing than a freelancer who would write the same article directly for the same publication where it will ultimately appear.

In-House Publications: Big companies have employees scattered all over the continent—and all over the world. These people must know about decisions affecting everything from their benefit programs to changes in corporate leadership. It is much cheaper for your business client to create a printed or videotaped piece and send it out than to assemble hundreds of people for a meeting to share information.

Business-to-Business Communications: One business often needs to let another business know what they're doing. They have ideas to share, products to promote, or people with information that needs to be communicated. Usually one company is trying to sell another something, and they need an effective way of doing it. A writer is required.

Direct Mail and Telemarketing: Telemarketing is the use of the telephone to follow up on direct mail or as a marketing tool itself. Telephone scripts must be written, right down to the last question and answer, for the callers to use on their prospective customers. This method of getting a message to select individuals is booming.

With new ways of zeroing in on target audiences, direct mail can also be a very effective means of getting to someone with the power to make the decision to buy. Direct mail can be a lot of fun, and a great deal of theatricalized tension can build around a big mailing deadline. Then there's more excitement as the responses come back.

Case Studies: These offer a great chance to work travel into your writing. Companies need written evaluations on how their products work in the field. You will be paid to go to a place where their product is being used and study it. The resulting survey helps them better adapt their products to the customers' needs. It also helps their sales reps know what the customer wants.

Training Materials: With so many new and complicated products coming out all the time, it's essential to be able to instruct people about how to use them. Microcomputers are a perfect example. When they came out, they were selling like hot cakes. Everyone had to have one. Unfortunately there were poorly organized training manuals for many computers, and the companies who couldn't train users easily often didn't make it. Training programs, manuals, and other materials have to be written and updated continually.

Training is essential for sales reps representing new products, too. The capabilities of new products need to be explained without hauling all those concerned into the company laboratories to show them how they work. Sales techniques need to be explained. Whatever form training materials take, a writer is needed to pull the details together.

Technical Documentation: Writers are needed for manuals on even simple equipment. User manuals are required for everything from household lawn mowers to sensitive medical equipment. A good freelance business writer takes confusing technical jargon and translates it into down-to-earth language the average reader can understand.

New Product Introduction: You may be hired to start from the very beginnings of a new product. First you name it, then write the marketing and advertising to let people know about it. The development of all sorts of printed materials comes with an assignment like this.

Audio-Visual Presentations: Slide shows (using one projector or 50) and videotaped presentations require scripts. Script assignments can send you across town or across the country with a crew to conduct interviews and research. Programs vary from 30-second television commercials to longer tapes on products and services.

Collateral Materials: These printed pieces accompany other promotional materials. Collateral writing assignment might be a simple brochure that you produce independent of an advertising campaign being handled by an ad agency.

There's no way to list the variety of writing opportunities businesses offer. There is literally no limit to what a writer can be called in to do. Anything can happen. At any time. Strange connections between people can network you into a writing adventure with a very unusual and interesting assignment. The whole time you're being paid for your writing. Paid well. And people are counting on you. They respect what you have to tell them, because they see you as an outside consultant.

Chapter 2

Understanding and Working for Corporations

Corporations are A-literate

Even many of the competent and powerful are helpless when compelled to put words on paper. This creates your opportunity to make money writing for corporations.

Business is hurting. Corporations have spent billions changing their offices to accommodate computers and enter the age of information. Most employees have access to word processing systems. They need to review tons of data every day to stay competitive. Their employees have thousands of pages of reports to read and interpret. But often they cannot read or write very well.

The amount of information any one corporate employee is theoretically responsible for reading is huge. The computers that were to have streamlined paperwork have actually added greatly to it. With all this information coming at them, you'd assume it is commonplace to have speedreaders sitting at every desk. Brilliant executives should be sitting there scanning written material for critical information, skillfully criticizing the content as they go. In response, their memos and directives should be quickly written and very concise.

This is not what is happening in corporations today.

Little, if any, time is set aside to read or write. Stroll down the halls of any corporation. You never see anyone poring through the newspaper or reading a report, though the information in these sources may be important to the business decisions they will make that day. If they read, it has to be during breaks or at lunch.

Reading is an activity corporations don't understand. Reading is made difficult by the sheer volume of information that is sent to people. There's no way for people to tell what's really important and needs attention, and what should be ignored. Much of what they have to read is too long, never gets to the point, or has nothing to do with their job.

If employees see other employees reading, they generally suspect them of wasting time. Seeing someone reading or writing in a corporate setting is not a common sight.

What is perceived as work to fellow corporate workers is talking on the telephone. Appearance is more important than substance. Walking around the corporate corridors with a piece of paper in your hand makes you look like you're doing something. When employees are seen walking between offices without something in their hands, it is assumed they are loitering. Making a good impression in a big company is more important for employees than communicating well-written information.

Writing presents another whole problem. People are shuffled through some business management courses having written little more than a three-page language competency test. It is really true that there are people in corporations in charge of vast projects, upon whom millions in corporate earnings depend, who have written nothing longer than a letter home from summer camp.

And they did that two decades ago. In pencil.

Setting pen to paper or fingers to word processor doesn't happen enough. Often an executive dictates into a machine. From that tape, a far more literate secretary types what was spoken. The secretary will often rewrite the draft copy before returning it for changes. The assumption is that someone in a powerful, executive position doesn't have to know how to relate information effectively in one of the most primary forms of communication—writing.

They can speak the words and that's enough. They never have to make the transition of words to paper, or written words to thought. A lot of papers get shuffled around, but the important things happen orally. Corporations are a-literate. The people in them have basic literacy, but don't practice their reading or writing effectively on the job.

I know a bright woman who moved into the corporate world from graduate school. Things went well for her. One promotion led to another, and soon she had her own secretary, office, and a clear path to the corporation's higher echelons.

Once during a meeting we were going through papers on her desk. On top was a draft of a letter she had pounded out on the type of an advanced correcting typewriter provided to most of her company's employees. The letter was full of errors, though she had gone through and corrected most of them with a pencil.

"Oh, my secretary types a clean draft of these things for me. I just indicate the changes and it comes out perfect," she explained matter-of-factly.

She asked me to read through the letter before it was sent to the secretary. The correspondence was relatively important. If it was misunderstood, hours and hours of peoples' time and a fair amount of money would be misspent.

The letter was terrible. It didn't even warrant being called a rough draft. She had trouble getting to the point. The corrections were haphazardly made. I couldn't tell if she didn't care that she had missed errors or didn't know any better.

The kicker was the two notations in the corrections. Two words were circled with a "sp" written beside them.

"What are these for?" I asked innocently, suspecting the worst.

"Those are notes for my secretary. I wasn't sure if those words were spelled correctly, so I circled them and she'll look them up."

I was flabbergasted. This up-and-coming corporate executive wouldn't even check her own spelling when she suspected a mistake. How would she ever learn the correct spelling? How could she claim authorship of what she wrote? How could there be any pride or sense of accomplishment in creating that communication?

The problem with business communications is that there is so little care taken in their preparation. People in corporations don't read or write. They don't feel they have the time.

Twenty-five million American adults can't read something as straightforward as a poison warning label. Studies say that one third of the people in the United States are illiterate. They can't read a simple book. In the number of books read per capita, the U.S. is 24th in the world.

I can't claim that one third of corporate employees are illiterate, too. It would make sense that this number would be much smaller, since it would be difficult to function in a corporation today without being able to read to some extent.

Or would it?

Corporations are not fortresses of egalitarian ideals. They are places for people to hide out. Many, many people in corporations do nothing more than show up for work in the morning and let the years roll by.

I believe that one of the basic problems is that people in businesses are not given the time to practice writing or to sit down and read. A high enough level of importance is simply not placed on reading or writing.

A manager of a large department in a Fortune 500 Company has over 50 people reporting to him. A budget of over four-million dollars is at his disposal. It takes this executive an entire day to write a simple one-paragraph memo. If his writing process is interrupted—as often happens—the first draft alone can take an entire week to complete.

This man is not stupid. His management skills are good, and he expresses himself well when speaking.

The problem comes when he is confronted with a blank page and the seemingly impossible task of committing his thoughts to written words. The result appears so permanent and important that it becomes too overwhelming a process to tackle.

These are the businesses our families rely on for employment. They are the corporations that drive our economy, filling the world with products to help us live better. They have loaded their offices with computer equipment to help them speed communications—but they don't know how to get their message across. The computer information networks, so highly touted as information conduits, are like empty pipelines. There is nothing of substance to send from one terminal to another besides production numbers and costs.

This is where you come in. Corporations are in dire need of skilled writing help from the outside. They desperately need people who can organize ideas and get information across in words.

They are willing to pay well for these services.

There is little sign that this a-literate state in corporations will change soon. The current thrust in schools to emphasize reading and writing will certainly help in years to come. But we can't wait 25 years for these youngsters to move up.

The writing help is needed right now. Freelance writers are going to continue to be essential to corporations for decades. They will gain in visibility as more and more of us move into the field.

Submerging Your Opinions

Most of your writing life you've been trained to either report facts or express your feelings. Business writing is something in between.

You had to learn to detail facts when the science teacher wanted a report. The journalism teacher wanted information in order of its importance. And he wanted to be able to shorten the length of what you wrote by cutting from the bottom without having to bother to read it.

On the other hand, your English teacher wanted to know what you really thought. After having you work through *Great Expectations* or *Moby Dick*, the assignment was to write in 500 words or less your impression of the classic masterpiece.

Students always protested, "Five hundred words! That's practically an entire encyclopedia. I can't think of that many words."

My 11th-grade English teacher, Mr. Wiley Shaver, summed it up best. "You can't even say 'good morning' in 500 words."

He was right, but most people never find that out for themselves.

The difference between other types of writing and business writing, is that people don't care what you think. They're interested in seeing if you can get their point across for them.

Functioning as an Outsider in a Corporation

There is no reason to be intimidated by a corporation. Some headquarters settings are arranged to be impressive. Giant buildings are designed to make you walk up an incline to a massive desk where a receptionist sits. She phones up the fact that you've arrived. Then you wait for someone to come and escort you in. This is all a very subtle form of intimidation.

Actually, corporations are filled with just plain people. Most of them are there because of the security a big company offers. They use that sense of security to strive and be great, or they use it to blend in.

Your first impression of a company from the inside will come from the offices, the uniformity of the people, and the massive bureaucratic structure they work under.

It's easy to overcome these initial potentially overwhelming impressions. Whenever confronted by a group of corporate people in their conservative suits and ties, just imagine them in casual clothes, jeans and T-shirts.

If someone is being particularly difficult, imagine them wearing giant diapers. If they're acting like children, think of them as children.

But treat them as adults.

The Corporate Profit Motive

More than anything else, a corporation is in the business of making a profit. They have to make money or they can't survive. Their nature is to make money. Their primary objective is to make money. You are being hired by them to write so they can make more money.

Get the picture?

But you are going to work with people in corporations who can't balance their own check books. You are going to get assignments to write for people who had to have their parents help them buy their cars. They've never made a purchase on their own that is larger than a bag of groceries. What they understand about the relative "value of things" is limited to their knowledge of weighing cantaloupes.

Coping with Committee Meetings

A corporation's actions are based on meetings. People often meet for no other reason than to keep track of what others in the company are doing. It's likely you will receive assignments at a committee meeting or have what you've written reviewed by a committee.

Resist this. Ask that the number of people present at any meeting be limited to two besides yourself. More than two people giving you direction or criticism wastes time. Committees with a lot of people make weak decisions. Individually, no one fully approves of what is decided by the group and seldom will any of them stand behind the consensus decision.

They say that the camel was designed by a committee trying to invent a horse.

A clear thinking client of mine has a pheasant farm that takes up all his spare time and keeps him sane. He is able to speak up in a meeting when too much conflicting input carries the conversation in ten directions at once. He says, "I think we're making a camel here. Let's turn over the information we have to the writer and let him figure it out."

Three cheers.

One corporate client I worked with needed to produce a lot of printed pieces for a company's marketing program. He needed brochures, specification sheets, booklets and much more. Instead of having me write the pieces and take the typed copy to a committee for a decision on any revisions, he had the copy I wrote typeset and made up into a complete layout. He figured that any changes made would be very expensive so the reviewers would refrain from making them.

As the freelance writer, I knew the products in this company better than many of the people working there, since I had information about the products from all areas of the company, not just the narrow area any one person was involved in. Because I had the ability to circulate through all the departments and get information they couldn't, I knew things they didn't. This background let me coordinate information from everywhere.

While this helped me get the writing done fast, it ruffled some feathers. People who work for a company don't like being told their information is insufficient, incomplete, or wrong.

During the course of the projects, there were times when people suspected and resented that I knew more than they did about their products. They were very angry. Some of them. I had to carefully take them aside and tell them what a tough spot I was in, trying to pull all this material together. I explained that everyone in the place had a different way of looking at things. Once they understood I meant well, everything was fine.

Writer in a Strange Land—How to "Merge"

Most persons interested in a writing career come out of a university environment. A liberal or applied arts background is very common.

Universities have the reputation for being kicked back and comfortable. The image of tweed jackets, scuffed shoes, and a rumpled tie are paramount to the success of an English professor. A student, especially a graduate student, must emulate the higher-ups. This is done either because he or she wants to have an intellectual look or just can't afford any better.

The environment inside a corporation is very unfamiliar to those who've never been exposed to it. It is the opposite of an academic setting. The corporate attitudes you've heard so much about are real. People dress in a standardized corporate style, talk a corporate language, and often live their lives within the narrow options presented by their company. Whoever said uniforms and regimentation are unique to the military?

Your ability to recognize these patterns and fit into them will make a difference in your freelance writing success.

Here are some pointers:

• You may have to wear an identification badge when you are admitted into an office. Don't clip this security badge to your front coat pocket. This makes you stick out as a visitor and an outsider to corporate culture. Stick it on a side pocket or on your purse or attache case. Hide your visitor badge.

• It's OK to dress slightly more relaxed and comfortably than your clients. The university tweed look is fine, but stick with the general type of clothes everyone in the corporation is wearing. Never show up in overly casual clothes, no matter how well you know the client.

• Don't tell people you're inexperienced. If you don't have a big portfolio of materials, take in what you do have. Include things you helped write, research or edit. Don't lie about your role in their production, but show your full range of skills.

• Sometimes it's better to show up without a portfolio and tell the potential client you forgot to bring it. Then talk your way through the meeting, asking all about their business. This way the focus is on you.

•I included materials from a political campaign I worked on in my first portfolio. The work was not entirely my own, though I collaborated on it. I replaced these samples with new ones as soon as I could. You can get writing credits by working on things like political campaigns, but shy away from them. Political materials tend to stir up emotions in some people. You never know if a client supported your candidate until it's too late. Your ability to write may be subordinated to your choice of the "wrong" party.

• Don't compete against yourself. I got caught once quite by accident. In a prospective client's office, I was chatting about the type of work I could do. I found that the client had a budget for a small slide show. I expressed an interest and estimated my charges for handling the project. Before I knew it, she had asked for bids from two audio-visual production companies for whom I also did work—or wanted to. Plus, she told the A.V. companies I was bidding against them on the project.

She had put me in the position of competing against people I wanted to work for. They were understandably upset. I had to withdraw from consideration on the project and send a copy of the letter stating this to the production companies.

• When you're on the outside of a company, you can have more clout than an on-staff employee. Even if you used to work for the company, you'll find that the fact you have the gumption to freelance and work on the outside gives you more influence in the structured corporate way of looking at things.

Likewise, a corporate client is usually looking for you to be aggressive and take ideas and go beyond the original concept. You often have to contribute to the creativity and bring to life a subject that may not be very interesting.

• Don't tell business clients you're just freelance writing while looking for a "real job." They don't want to familiarize you with their products and establish you as a vendor (supplier of a service), then find you're off working full time someplace else. This is a growing complaint among many business clients. They invest time to locate a good freelance writer, only to find the writer is only coasting between permanent jobs and is not available for their next project.

Understanding Corporate Structure

An exciting aspect of business writing is that it can take you into very exotic and fascinating places. You can leap from doing a video tape script about floor cleaning in a warehouse to interviewing the new CEO of a Fortune 500 company.

There can be swift movement between the two projects and often little reason why one potential assignment will come through and another won't. No telling where a casual phone call from a client will send you.

A reason many of us write is for the credit we receive. It's tough to take credit for what you've done in business writing. Some clients don't associate the freelance writer with previous successful projects. So every time you go to a company, whether it's the second or fifteenth time, you must talk to the people who make the decisions and remind them that you have already been a great help.

There are several ways to make contact with the right person in a company. Your best approach has to do with your personality, and cultivating what is positive about it. Little of it has to do with your writing at first.

Begin making contact by understanding the hierarchy.

Corporations usually segment people into three layers. At the base of the structure are the real workers. There are the secretaries, beginning level managers, and the people who have to grind out the work day after day. These folks have to get things done. Their positions don't allow them to put their work off because it's too obvious when they don't get things accomplished.

I couldn't believe my first year of exposure to the corporate environment. To have secretaries available and retyping things for us while in the middle of a meeting was mind-boggling. This will be especially enlightening to you if you've been pounding out a novel, play or some other writing of your own. You've done all the work by yourself in the solitude of your own kitchen. It's easy to feel that writing is something you do all on your own with no help from anyone else. This sort of thing just doesn't take place in a corporation.

It was amazing to find that a secretary really would go get coffee for everyone in a meeting. More amazing yet was that their bosses were just as willing to get coffee for secretaries when it was appropriate. Suddenly the lonely writer is surrounded by all sorts of people when coming to a business to get an assignment.

You will get used to the corporate environment, but if you come from an academic background with the usual presumptions about the way things ought to be done and the routine in universities, it is disquieting at first.

You will find that once you've cultivated friendships with the basic level people, you can enjoy your relationship with them more than any other group within the company. You can make one another's work easier. They can get messages through to managers for you and do small favors that can make your writing life go much more smoothly.

The next level of people are the middle managers. You often see them in New Yorker cartoons, trudging through the day.

Middle managers are in tough positions. They have a lot of responsibility, but only enough authority to do things specifically structured into their jobs. Real authority is doled out on a limited basis. The amount of authority—or power to make things happen—varies greatly from individuals who have the freedom to do whatever they want to those who have to run to a boss to get approval on everything and drag you through a bunch of meetings to get go-aheads.

One definition of middle managers is "executives who put off making decisions until that decision makes itself." They don't actually have to decide anything, since that would be too threatening. And their main goal at work is to keep their position in the company safe and secure. So they let things go until whatever happens, happens. What happens is usually very arbitrary.

Ideally, you want to work for a manager who can make decisions and take responsibility for them. However, you're very apt to be working for middle managers when you do freelance business writing, and decision-making is not what you'll generally find in middle management.

The third level is upper management. As a freelance writer, you are going to deal directly with these people only occasionally. You will use them as resource people. You'll call on them for information you can't get anywhere else in the company. Upper management may drop by a meeting once in a while, but for the most part they view managing a freelance writer as a middle level function.

Always treat upper management people with kid gloves. They are your client's bosses, so give the best impression possible. This may include saying complimentary things about your client to them. Not gushing—just being positive about the person. Do this by making it clear your client has made the best decision possible in hiring you. I'm not kidding about this—dumb as it sounds. It works. Also mention all the responsibility and hard work being undertaken in the project you're working on.

This seems like brown-nosing. It really isn't. Upper management people are easily detached from the day-to-day activities of their organizations. But they do want to be informed of what's going on. And they want to know that the people who work for them are doing a good job, since it reflects back on them and affects their job reviews.

Once you've been in enough business settings, you'll come to recognize who is doing the work and who is just pretending to be busy. And which ones can't even tell the difference themselves. You'll know the people who can help you get assignments and who can help you finish writing projects on time and with the best possible quality.

The Corporate State of Mind

Know what a company is like and half the battle of writing successfully for that company is won.

Business people work long hours.

Not only does a person working for a corporation have to report to work at a specific time, but they eat lunch at the same time everyone else does. Hungry or not. Their work pace is often set by others and there is little opportunity to break out of the character mold set by the company. The nature of this corporate character can vary from peaceful self-satisfaction to constant fear of making a minor mistake, much less a real decision.

Because you freelance for a living, many people who work for corporations are going to be slightly jealous of you. This is natural. Everyone would like to break out and be their own boss. They'll tell you you're lucky because you don't have a boss. They don't realize that a freelance writer doesn't have just one boss. There is a different boss for each project. You have thousands of bosses.

The attitude that a freelance writer leads a carefree life works against you, because you're treated as though you can take care of yourself under any circumstance. Little consideration is given to your basic needs—like paying your mortgage on the due date. It can also work for you, since people in companies want contact with writers on the outside to help them get a fresh approach to their own work.

Because you look like a free spirit, people in corporations don't understand that you're not only serious about writing for them, but you want to run your writing as a successful business.

It's typical that they feel you are overpaid. This is because they seldom realize you're operating a business and have to pay for things their corporation provides for them without cost. The people you work for get free medical coverage and life insurance. They are given an office, desk, and all the office supplies they need. Their environment is well lit and ventilated. A telephone with all the long distance time they need is provided without charge.

If you want these things for your business, you have to pay for them yourself.

Point this out to people if you need to. They are often so caught up in their corporate ways of doing things that they forget that some of us earn a living in very different ways than they do. All of your needs are not provided for by a benevolent corporation.

Chapter 3

Finding Your Business Markets

Full or Part Time?

Freelance business writing can be a full-time occupation if you want it to be. It can take as many hours of your day as you're willing to invest in it. You may come to feel that you shouldn't refuse any assignment. You can get so tired and overworked your face hurts. With me, that's a sure sign I'm putting in too much work time.

You can, also, cut the amount of work you accept to any level you want. Part-time business writing is fine, if you can live on it. The only problem is that the fewer clients you have the less certain your income and the more erratic your work schedule. Sometimes you'll have too much to handle for a week, then absolutely nothing to do for a couple months. This is an obvious time for your personal writing.

There's no easy way to settle into a schedule. It's going to change every week, probably every hour. In fact, probably one of the reasons you decided to go into freelance writing is your dislike for schedules that are too inflexible.

Naturally there's a trade-off. No matter how heavy or light your work load, there is a constant tension that accompanies it. Everything was due yesterday. Budgets are never big enough. The clients feel insecure about their jobs and pass that stress along to you. They think the last writer made a mess of the project, so you'd better do it right. Or maybe they "just know" that you and all other writers are too expensive.

These are things you're going to hear, whether you're working full or part time. It will all add to the undercurrent of tension you will feel, but which you can learn to live with.

Evaluating Your Market Potential

To freelance for business, begin by evaluating your market. Find out if it will support you.

You can write for business part time practically anywhere in the world. There are companies just down the street from you who need writing help and can afford to hire you. It may just be a matter of your dropping by and making your availability known, or it may involve calling, following up, and really having to work at getting assignments.

Go to any medium-sized city's downtown. Stand on a street corner and look up at the buildings. Hidden up amongst all those little windows is someone who needs a brochure or press release.

Now sit down and look at a map of your town. Circle all the Fortune 1000 companies. Fortune magazine publishes a list of the largest industrial companies every year. If there are none, how about in nearby towns?

Go through an area chamber of commerce directory and find companies who sell products. Companies that gross at least $100 million are most likely to have sufficient need for your services on a regular basis. Then list all the service companies, such as banks, brokerage firms, and insurance companies of any size.

This will let you begin to get a general picture of your business writing opportunities.

Find out how many advertising agencies are servicing your region. The more ad agencies and public relations firms, the better for you. This indicates there are vast opportunities out there. And it shows there is a healthy competition between freelance writers. This is great, since your clients will be better educated about their needs and more likely to recognize good writing. They'll be more apt to know what they want and to be easier to work with. Where there is a lot of activity, the mechanisms are set up within your clients' organizations for paying freelancers. So you get your checks faster.

Checking Out the Competition

It's important to know who the other writers are in your primary market area. This serves several purposes. First it assures you that other people are supporting themselves through their freelance writing. Also, it can give you someone to compare notes with.

You can meet with the other freelance business writers to learn who deadbeat clients are—and avoid the problems they can bring you. These contacts will help you find out who's not paying bills or who is difficult to work with. Understandably, it is less likely that you're going to hear who are good clients that pay well.

Ask other freelance writers, graphic designers, and people in related advertising and marketing fields if they're making a good living and how they're doing it. Don't ask for help in getting work. You aren't going to get good information from someone who thinks you're trying to compete with him.

Also, seek out people doing the type of business writing you want to do. Begin with a phone calls to freelancers to establish the fact that what they do is the kind of writing you are interested in.

I made a mistake early on. It had been suggested to me that I contact an older, well-established business writer. This person had been freelancing for years and his name was practically a part of community folklore.

I left a message for him and received a call back. Not knowing who I was, he likely thought I was offering him an assignment. I introduced myself and told him I was beginning a career as a freelance business writer. I asked if he could give me any advice on how to get started. It was as if I'd asked for his client list. I was immediately unwelcome on the phone. He curtly announced, "I don't know how you'd get started in writing these days. It's terribly hard. Essentially impossible."

"Yes, sir. However, this really is what I want to do. I'm sure I can make a success of it. Maybe you could at least tell me who to ask for assignments." I asked as nicely as I could. (I didn't know this was not the proper approach.)

"I have no idea," he said. His voice growing even less tolerant. He was clearly out to discourage me, lest I add to the number of writers out pounding the pavement and stealing his assignments. He was an older man with established accounts he wanted to retain. He was not ready to start over with new clients. If some upstart writer came along with lower rates and more energy, he didn't want to encourage him as a competitor.

"You must get assignments constantly," I tried to continue the faltering conversation. "Do you get writing projects you don't want to handle yourself that you could send in my direction?" I politely inquired. To me it made sense to ask, since I could be doing him a favor by taking a load off his back.

"That never happens," he said, ending the call. And that was the extent of my contact with this living legend. When contacting the competition, expect to be greeted by a wide range of responses. Learn to filter these to determine who will help you with information and who is so insecure about their own freelance business writing career that they try to thin the ranks.

Search for good, healthy, well-balanced people to give you input. Make friends with them and stay in touch. Watch out for freelancers who aren't as serious as you—or who are too serious.

I have a friend who's been freelancing for years. This person loves to hang on the phone and chat for hours. Gossiping about the people in the marketing and advertising business is a major activity for her. Phone conversations exceed time spent writing by several hundred percent.

I used to meet with her occasionally. After many sessions over lunch being told how to go about making a living in the writing business, we got too familiar. The amount of time spent gossiping got larger and larger. The useful conversation about freelance writing completely disappeared. The result was I had to back off from our friendship.

Eventually, when I had a problem getting paid by a client, my freelance writer friend got hooked into the gossip of the situation. Her gossiping back and forth greatly complicated and delayed my collecting the past due bill.

Overall, locating and getting to know other writers can be a great help. One gave me some valuable tips about getting into a big multinational company. Another was anxious to help me avoid mistakes in ordering certain word processing software. And still another freelance business writer gave me a good system for evaluating advertising agencies. By examining their yearly gross income, I could determine which were more likely to use freelancers.

The very small ad agencies do their writing themselves. So do the largest ones. Get a list of ad agencies in town and look at the middle of the listing by yearly revenue. The agencies in the middle range of revenues are often too large to handle everything in house. To survive, they have to go outside and use freelance writers' talents. You'll get a feel for what size agency can give you work after approaching several different ones and gauging the results.

I have a woman friend who became an acquaintance through a small print shop. Her one-person public relations firm doesn't really compete with my freelance business writing. Because of this she is an ideal person to get together with for lunch occasionally and chat about our businesses, although no real solid leads come out of the conversations with her. It is good, though, to talk with someone who shares similar obstacles in her work. I've never seen an example of her work, nor do I know how she deals with clients. It's easy to assume she produces good solid stuff. Her attitude is up front and she works hard. The business relationships she cultivates seem positive and professional.

By establishing these kinds of contacts and developing friends in marketing, advertising, and business communications, you will more easily maintain your balance in this turbulent profession. When a client is giving you a bad time, you will better understand what they're really thinking. When you have a success in a project, a good friend in the business—especially one you seldom work with—will help keep you humble.

I get several calls a month from people asking advice about getting into freelance writing. I'm helpful to a point, giving them some of the basics, but I always tell them how tough it can be. When they ask me for help getting assignments, that shuts me off fast. Don't give away work to your competition.

Once you're established and someone calls you for advice, you can be friendly but vague. Don't ever discourage anyone since you wouldn't want that kind of treatment yourself. Just don't tell all your secrets.

Going Outside Your Area

You can also go outside your immediate geographic area when looking for work. This is relatively easy if you have a specialty. Commuting to their office should be an additional charge, and they should be quite willing to pay well for your expertise. This includes their picking up extra expenses: phone calls, lunches, etc.

Getting in touch with people outside the immediate area can be done in many ways. Writing letters is modestly effective. Telephone contact is the best, but can be expensive. Referrals are likely to be the best way in, though the process is slow and unpredictable. Look for clients outside your region who are specialized in a field you have the capacity for serving and who are large enough to supply you with steady work. There's no use working to get an out of town client who only uses you once a year.

You can also contact corporate public relations departments of companies headquartered in other cities to see if they need articles or information about their operations where you live. These might be branch offices, distributors, or research facilities.

Traveling the World and Getting Paid For It

Decide where in the world you want to travel. Outline a proposed itinerary and find out which corporations have sales offices, branches, plants or subsidiaries where you're going. If you're going to Rio, check out what companies have offices in Brazil. If London or Rome is where you're going, see who has a sales office or manufactures products in Europe.

Public relations and other departments are often anxious to get stories about their company activities and personnel in distant locations. They want to take advantage of a freelance writer who is going anyway, so they are not charged for getting you there, only for the cost of the article. They save greatly. They may have been thinking about doing an article about a new employee who has been sent to the place you will be going. There is the possibility that a new plant has opened and no one back home knows what it's really like.

Employees in one part of the world are interested in their counterparts abroad, so human interest stories are always possible.

For example, a company may manufacture a raw film product in Spain. The material is then shipped to Kansas for final processing. The workers on either end of the process would like to know about the others. An in-house publication could likely use a story like this. You would have the assignment before you leave on the trip and could count on the income when you get back.

I frequently take trips within the U.S. Every time I go, I contact a variety of clients to see if they have special writing needs at my destination. I seldom go anywhere without some success in landing at least one writing assignment.

This makes a portion of the travel expenses a deductible business expense. Check with your accountant to determine exactly what you can write off when traveling.

At one point I wanted to see Japan and Hong Kong. I planned a two-week trip, then went to clients for assignments. The trip began by flying to Narita, Tokyo's international airport.

There was a World Exposition north of Tokyo, so I was able to get a press pass admitting me free-of-charge to all the exhibits. I wrote about the exposition for my local paper. I also arranged to write a piece about a product being used in several of the exhibits at the Expo. This product was manufactured by a company who wanted to report on it for an industry magazine. They paid me to write a story and took care of placing the finished article themselves.

My Asian trip continued with a Bullet Train ride to Koyoto, the ancient Japanese capital. The few days visit there was relaxing and I wrote an article on spec from the perspective of the first time traveler to the Orient. When I returned, I sold it to a smaller suburban newspaper.

From Japan I flew down to Hong Kong for a week. Practically every company in the world seems to have some presence in Hong Kong, even if it's only a mail drop or someone answering a phone. A big company I'd worked with regularly had a representative based there. The region he served extended north to Korea, southeast to New Zealand, and west to Thailand. I wrote a brief biography of his career that included his current duty station. The company used it in a division newsletter. I also interviewed the man about the products and services he provides this region. This turned into an article about how they sell to the Far East. The story was placed in industry publications, and

I was paid when I turned it in to the company, who placed the piece.

This sure beat sending out query letters, waiting for them to come back, sending in draft after draft of revisions, then getting paid a modest fee when the articles were published.

When I travel, I figure that breaking even on writing assignment income and expenses is what you can realistically expect. If that's enough to take you half way around the world, it's worth it. If you come out ahead, that's even better.

Staking Out Your Claim—and Working It

To get your own piece of the freelance business writing market, you have to decide you are going to succeed at it. Getting started isn't just a matter of jumping in with a big push. Staying with it and constantly working to expand your share of the market is essential to your continuing success.

Chapter 4

Getting Your Business Set Up

Thinking of Yourself as a Business

There are many benefits to being self-employed. Your time is your own. You meet new people all the time. The possibility of seeing new things and visiting interesting places is always there. You take along a sense of freedom wherever you go.

Tell someone working for a company you are a freelance writer and they wonder how you do it. They're curious about your clients and the process you follow to get the words out. It seems to others like a fabulous occupation.

They don't think about some of the disadvantages and don't realize you have to pay your own health insurance, manage your own retirement plan, and provide many of the things a corporation automatically, and invisibly, gives their employees. These benefits routinely amount to an additional 25 to 40% over a corporate employee's stated salary.

A freelance writer has to go out and buy these same benefits on the open market. As an individual, you can sometimes hook into a group insurance plan through an organization. Most of the time you get the expensive rate because you have to buy these things alone.

Disability insurance comes in different packages. Payment is based on a yearly income that is a percentage of what you currently earn. The payments begin after your choice of an unreimbursed period of disability, usually 30, 60, or 90 days. The premium drops the longer you're willing to wait for that first disability check. Disability coverage is a very good idea once you have established your writing career, since your financial obligations tend to grow over time and need protection from a loss of income. Unless you've had substantial, regular income, however, few companies will issue this coverage for writers.

Something else you have to provide yourself is car insurance. If the car insurance people think you're using your car substantially for business, you might have to pay the same rate as laundry truck drivers. Delivery trucks and other commercial vehicles pay a much higher business rate because they're on the road constantly and their chances of an accident are consequently much higher. Even real estate agents are liable for higher car insurance because they carry customers and are on the road all the time.

Another financial hassle is proving income. When you go to the bank for a loan or to fill out the forms for a mortgage, the word "writer" on your application sends shudders up the loan officer's spine. The bank doesn't know how to judge the success of self-employed people in the first place. Worse, the fact that you'd admit to being a writer creates the image in their mind of people who spend their days at sidewalk cafes drinking and chatting with passersby.

Buttoned-up bankers assume it is impossible to earn a decent income, or for you to be at all responsible about paying your bills, when you call yourself a "writer." Even if you are a very responsible person, the fact that you're a writer may severely handicap you.

These prejudices are very real. You'll run into them when you shop for insurance or loans.

There is an approach to applying for these types of financial instruments that can reduce your costs. Realize that when you are a freelance business writer you do much more than just write. Although your writing is usually what the client ultimately wants from the business transaction, you are much more than that. Getting a project finished requires you to know about public relations. You must understand how the company wishes to project itself, and you have to understand whatever technical data are included. Overall, your skills at marketing must be good. Many consultants hired by companies end up responsible for writing. These consultants are no different from you or me. They are simply able to charge more for their time because they've tacked the title "consultant" onto their business card. They don't just call themselves "writer." There is no degree any University grants that gives these people the title "consultant." No foundation or organization awards them that title. Tests don't have to be passed.

The same is true about the name "writer." You may call yourself a "writer" even if you have never struck a typewriter key.

However, a funny thing happens when a mortgage lender or disability insurance sales rep sees the word "consultant" in the slot named "occupation" on an application. The image of the starving writer vaporizes, and the image of a reliable upstanding citizen is created.

When you freelance for corporations, you are—for all intents and purposes—a marketing consultant. If you write PR, you are a public relations consultant. And if you decide to be something else because of your specialty, you may be an advertising consultant, media consultant, business communications consultant, corporate communications consultant, or any other type of consultant you wish.

There is no difference between what you do as a freelance business writer and what anyone else does with a consulting title. Corporations react to the consultant title, too, with more reverence, and they're likely to pay a consultant more than a writer.

It is a strange misunderstanding, the difference between the two. A consultant is just a writer with opinions that don't have to be committed to paper. Once versed in the business environment, you'll have just as many good ideas, and these will be a part of what you provide your client. Plus, your opinions are likely to be more practical than those of a pure consultant because you have to make yours work.

Finally, do you really want to *be* a consultant? No way. We all want to be writers forever and hate to think that our title—writer—will be replaced with a trendy consulting title. So be a writer. But remember what banks, insurance companies, and other institutions want to hear. Calling yourself a consultant occasionally is one honest way to work with them to save yourself money.

The Basics

There are a few things you must pick up before launching your freelance career. Here are ten things to consider:

1. A word processor with letter quality printer or correcting typewriter. Old dot matrix printers were too hard to read, but some of the new ones produce very acceptable print. Be sure it looks as much as possible like typed copy.

2. Answering machine. The type with capability to play back messages when you phone in from distant places. Outgoing message tape length should be 10 seconds. Any longer and you'll get too many hang ups—and bore the people who call often. Most machines have removable cassettes that allow you to vary message length. Incoming message length should be unlimited. Make sure you tell people to listen for the beep, and don't make a recording that answers with a cute message. Keep it straight forward and business-like. New clients may get their first impression of you from your recorded message.

3. Business cards. Standard business cards can be printed overnight. Get yours designed by a good graphic artist. They should read horizontally, so they fit into standard Rolodex files. Vertically formatted cards can be eye catching, but impossible to file. So are double cards that fold to the standard size. Your business card is the most important part of your "stationery" package.

4. Stationery and forms. Get to know a good designer and have your stationery designed. You need: Letterhead, invoice, package labels, and envelopes. A consistent style should tie them together so that any correspondence from you is immediately recognizable.

5. Accountant. Find one by referral from freelancers in related fields. Interview the accountant to make sure you're compatible. If there's the slightest doubt that you won't be comfortable with the accountant, talk to more until you find one that you're happy with.

6. Lawyer. Get to know a lawyer with experience in handling the problems of self-employed people. Issues your lawyer can help you resolve are everything from incorporation of your business to tax advice and other matters—including help in getting payment for your bills.

7. Wardrobe that lets you approximately match the appearance of your clients.

8. Pocket appointment book. Find a calendar system that displays an entire week. These are made by many different companies, some being much easier to use than others. Look for a calendar with removable address pages in the back. Each year you can transfer the address section to the new calendar, without having to copy it over.

9. Subscriptions and reference books. Depending on your work, you may need special dictionaries and reference books. Make sure to have Strunk and White's *The Elements of Style*. Also get the *AP Style Book* and a number of dictionaries. Visit several well stocked bookstores and compare the entries for the same words in different dictionaries. You'll be surprised at how they vary. Build your supply of reference books so you can eventually cover any question.

10. Transportation, messengers and communications. Getting yourself and your materials around is paramount. New York may be the only U.S. city where you can do this without a car. Everywhere else an appropriate vehicle is essential to getting you to your clients on time. For sending written materials, messenger services are available most places. Taxis will deliver packages, too, and are sometimes a good substitute for a dedicated courier service.

The telephone, obviously, is your most valuable communications equipment. Select a good quality phone with the options most helpful to you and sign up with the long distance service that offers clear calls, ease of getting through, and handily detailed billings.

Chapter 5

Terms and Things You Need to Know

Handy Glossary of Terms

Marketing, advertising, and all business communications can be terribly jargon-ridden with terminology that changes all the time.

One of my favorite activities in the freelance business writing environment is to ask someone who is boldly tossing around a new acronym or expression what they're talking about. So fearlessly do people adopt new idioms that these new words often become a part of the language, no matter how inappropriate they are.

Don't let people using unfamiliar terminology snow you. Sometimes they're doing it to hide their own lack of understanding. However, most people sincerely want you to understand what they're talking about, so they'll be pleased to explain terms you're unfamiliar with. If you don't understand something, ask.

A good way to familiarize yourself with the way things work in the corporate communications business—and to learn new terms—is to tour facilities of printers, graphic artists, photographers, photo separators, typesetters, and others. They usually have a lot of pride in their workplace and are pleased to show it off. Ask them anything you don't understand about what they're doing. A couple of visits to working studios are worth a long semester in a beginning graphic production class.

Here's a list of some business writing terms you should know. They are common and well accepted today. Your own glossary will quickly grow as you gain experience.

Audio-Visual: That group of communications tools such as videotapes, slide shows, laser videodiscs, film, computer-generated effects, and other media that combine visuals and sound (usually narration). You can write scripts for all types of audio-visual productions.

Art Director—Also Graphic Artist or Graphic Designer: The person responsible for the visual appearance of a business communications piece. Usually for a printed work, but also for the design of audio-visual programs, trade show booths, and other materials. Their responsibilities will differ from one project to the next. Sometimes they will only design the basic layout of the piece. Other times they will make sure the amount of copy you write is the correct length. They may ask you to revise copy or headlines to fit the space they've allotted. Often they'll work with a photographer, helping arrange the composition of the photos.

Body Copy or Text: The main information segment, usually in the smallest type and arranged in columns in a brochure.

Client: The individual or company you write for. Most often the client is the decision maker, okays what you write, and approves paying your invoices. The term *client* refers both to the *contact* person and the purchasing company itself.

Copy: This is what you write. Copy is the words that appear in everything from ads to brochures to anything else that is printed. It not only refers to any text that will be printed, but includes spoken words used in TV ads, radio spots, and elsewhere. Copy can be interchanged with the words "text," "words," or "writing."

Copywriter: The person who writes the copy. Advertising agencies identify their writers as copywriters. It is generally better to identify yourself as a "freelance writer", rather than a "copywriter", as the latter can appear to some clients to limit the scope of your writing interests and abilities to ads.

Desk Top Publishing: Using a computer to compose a piece on the video display screen, an operator can create a document ready for printing without having to work up a physical layout, set type, or have a keyline done. It's all done on a single "desk top."

Font: Printer's term for a given style of type (Helvetica, Gothic, etc.) all set in one size.

Headline: The largest line of type. This has to catch the readers' interest and draw them into the page. Usually at the top of the page, although the location can vary with the material.

The Hook: The theme, catch expression, or idea that "hooks" the readers and gets them to pay attention to what you're offering. Think of the hook as a theme to build your copy on.

Keyline: The type, illustrations, and all the other elements of the printed piece glued down on a heavy white board, usually in a graphic arts studio. The page is arranged exactly as it will appear when printed. The person who carefully arranges the pieces on the board is the keyliner. Some people specialize in this task; others do both the original design and the keyline.

Subhead: A headline that's in a smaller type size than the main headline but usually larger than the text. This might set off a chapter or indicate different subjects within the copy.

Typesetting: The photo-mechanical process where a computer-driven machine photographically produces type. These systems get more sophisticated all the time. An operator types in the words and sets the equipment to produce the type in a certain typeface of a specific size font. Your word processor may be able to send the text through a modem directly to the typesetting machine.

Type should always be very carefully proofed by several people before it is printed. It is not the writer's responsibility to proof the type, but it's a good idea to remind an inexperienced client to have it proofed for errors.

Agree to proof the type only if the client also reviews it and is ultimately responsible for its accuracy. You don't want to be saddled with a typesetting charge because of errors.

Photo Separation: A process for taking a full color photograph and separating it into its four basic colors for reproduction. With this done, the printer can print each of the four colors to create the full color photo accurately. Blue, yellow, red, and black are used in the four-color printing process.

Point: A unit of size of type equal to about 1/72 of an inch. Type is described as 10 point, 12 point, etc.

Screen: Color and black-and-white photos must be screened into tiny dots before printing. Screens are calibrated by size. Fewer, bigger dots are used for lower grade paper stock, such as newspapers. Smaller dots give a sharper image. Slick magazines tend to use a higher percentage screen to reproduce the photos with more dots—and more clarity.

Spec Type: Specify type style and size. Something the graphic artist does. He goes through your typed copy and indicates to the typesetter how words or sections of text should be set, indicating type style and point size.

Vendor: Anyone who offers a service to the client from outside the client's company. Vendors include writers, graphic artists, illustrators, printers, photographers and people in many other professions. You are a vendor to your client company. You may, in turn, hire other vendors to work with you to produce a finished writing product for a client.

Writing Copy For Print

When people in marketing communications say "print", they are talking about most anything that will be printed.

This means that the copy you write will be worked with by several people on its way to its final form.

To help your client understand how you want the copy to appear in the finished piece, and to tell the graphic artist how to put the copy into a design, several indications can be included in the copy you submit.

Begin by titling the first page of your copy and indicate which draft it is. You may have to go through several drafts before the copy is approved, so make sure to indicate whether it's a rough first, second, third or final draft.

Give all information for the graphic artist in parenthesis. First state the location of the copy. In the case of a brochure where you've seen the layout, indicate the page and its location.

Then label the headline, sub heads and text or body copy. I always list it as "text" because there are fewer letters to type. It will look something like this when you hand it in:

Sample:

NEW SERVICE TO BOAT OWNERS BROCHURE
SECOND DRAFT

(COVER)
(HEAD)

Boat Owners Save with Acme
Floating Dock Service

(INTERIOR BROCHURE LEFT)
(HEAD)

New Service Cleans Hulls Fast

(SUB HEAD)

First of Its Kind

(TEXT)
Today, boat owners can have boats that glide
through the water more smoothly than ever. Boat
hulls can be inexpensively cleaned by a fast,
new Acme Company product. The savings in time
and money can be enough to have the work done
three times as often.

This example very simply shows how to divide the
sections of what you write. There is no right or wrong way
to do this, just as there is no right or wrong way to write
resumes, press releases, AV scripts, speeches, or any other
kind of business writing—though many people will declare
their preferred way to be the only right way. However, your
client will probably prefer a certain style. You can develop
your own format for presenting copy and adapt it to your
clients' wishes as you go along.

Audio-Visual Scripts

The first thing to remember in scripting audio-visual
shows is that the visuals are what impact the viewer more
than any other aspect of the program. What is remembered
most is what is seen.

Secondary impact comes from the accompanying words.
When scripting A.V. presentations, whether they're video-
tape, video disc, film, slide shows, or something else, your
attention to the visual impact is of primary importance.

There is a big difference between writing for the eyes and writing for the ears. At the very least, it's a good idea to read your script aloud to hear how it sounds.

Many clients only do A.V. presentations occasionally. They will be unfamiliar with them and won't be able to visualize the images that the narrator's words support.

You can help them understand what you've written by carefully describing the visuals in your script. Help them imagine what they're going to see by describing what the accompanying image will be during your meetings with them.

The form for industrial scripts is different from other types of business writing. Two columns are used. The left column is what you see in the show. These are the visuals. The right column is the narrative, usually spoken.

An "on-camera" narrator is someone you see on the screen as they speak. The advantages to on-camera narration are that it provides a personal touch and it is easier to drive home information. Disadvantages are that it is more expensive to shoot this way and the narrator must be animated and dynamic. If you want to update the program later, it's difficult to make changes that match the original show.

In "voice-over" narration, the voice is heard but the narrator unseen. This method is less expensive to produce and allows the narration to be easily changed in later versions of the program as new information becomes available.

Here is an example of a standard script layout. Feel free to adapt any business writing format to suit the particular nature of your projects.

Sample:

<u>ACME HULL CLEANING PRODUCT VIDEO TAPE SCRIPT</u>

<u>THIRD DRAFT</u>

VISUALS	NARRATION
Open on boats at anchor. Small harbor with boat owners at work.	The private boat owner has many expenses. Keeping the hull free of debris is seldom a major concern, compared to more obvious tasks—such as mending the sails.

Focus on one boat owner and specific tasks. Follow the owner to stern of craft. See him pull up anchor, ready for cast off.	Did you realize how much money could be saved when a sail boat has a clean hull and moves more easily through the water?
Boat under sail with happy owner at helm.	It's easier to steer, and a great pleasure to spend a day under sail.

See how the visuals match the narration? Use your imagination to create an image for the viewer, one the director can create on the screen. Ask to see scripts the client has used before if possible. They'll give you an idea of the format and style expected.

Copyrights

When you sell writing to a company, it belongs to them. The only circumstances where your "work-for-hire" does not become the company's property is when you have made some other specific arrangement with them to release the rights to you. This is extremely unusual.

If there is a reason you want the rights to what you write, make sure to have that agreed to in advance, in writing. Be certain the terms of this agreement are signed by your client. To be triply certain, have your lawyer take a look at the document to make sure it does what you want it to do.

Another way to protect your the rights is when you are paid. On the back of the check, briefly write the terms already agreed to. For example: "All rights to written materials retained by the writer."

Again, check with your lawyer to make sure your agreement accomplishes what you want it to, and that it will continue to, long after you are paid by your client.

Little of what you write for business will be of any use to anyone except the client you create it for. To make sure your client's rights are protected, learn a few things about copyrights.

To help your client protect what you have written for them, ask if they'd like you to add a copyright to the end of your copy. This is indicated by a circle C, © symbol.

The laws currently allow protection of materials with the addition of this symbol at the end of a document or video tape with the words following it: ©—the year of publication, name of company.

For example: © 1990 Acme Corporation.

For complete protection, copies of the materials must be filed with the Library of Congress. There is a form for doing this, available from the Copyright Office, Library of Congress, Washington, D.C., 20559.

Sometimes the legal department of a corporation will review writing to see that is conforms to their concept of a litigation-free presentation.

Conservative lawyers who are busy protecting written works can make them practically unreadable. They can load them down with copyright marks and extra words to the point of exhaustion. It can make the reader feel that getting through your copy is like running hurdles.

Familiarize yourself with copyright rules. Ask clients how they protect their copyrights. You can get additional information from handouts available through the government printing office on copyright protection. Or from the legal staff at the corporation.

Use this information to protect your clients' publications. If they have a particular way of implementing their copyright, follow their instructions carefully, since your clients are ultimately responsible for the copy being correct.

Trademarks

Nothing can confuse a business more than figuring how to protect what it owns. Brand names are a major investment that need protecting. Millions in advertising dollars are poured into promoting a specific brand. If the name isn't protected, anyone can come along and use it.

A brand name is protected by a trademark. A trademark protects something valuable: a unique brand name.

Brand name protection has a long and disastrous history. Many of the names we use generically were once brand names, developed by companies to identify their specific products. Because they weren't properly protected, the name became generic. Escalator, thermos, elevator, aspirin, diesel, cola, yo-yo, dry ice and other names have lost their trademark protection. We know them now as the names of product types, not brand names that belong to any one company. An easy way to think of a trademark is as an adjective used to modify a noun.

Let's say the product you're writing about is a vacuum cleaner. *Vacuum cleaner* is a noun describing a product that many manufacturers make. We'll say your client is the Acme Company, manufacturers of fine vacuum cleaners for half a century. The name of their brand of vacuum cleaner is the Destroyer. Whenever the name *Destroyer* is used to describe their product, it must be followed by the noun *vacuum cleaner*. The Destroyer Vacuum Cleaner is a product of the Acme Company. *Destroyer* is a trademark of Acme Company and describes their brand of vacuum cleaner.

Generally speaking, the first use of a brand name in a document must have a trademark symbol or a registered trademark symbol following it. The trademark is indicated by a ™ symbol. The registered trademark is a ®, called a circle R.

The first use of a trademark in a document might be on the cover or in the first line of copy. Sometimes, the company will spell out the entire trademark situation at the end of the document. In an advertisement, it is common to find a list of the protected materials at the bottom. Rolls Royce, among other companies, carefully protects trademarks in its advertising, listing them at the bottom of every ad.

Study examples in brochures, ads, press releases and on product container labels to see how trademarks and registered trademarks are handled.

The difference between the ™ and ® is that the ™ has not been registered. When application for registration is made, a search is carried out to see that the name or symbol is not in use by anyone else. A ™ can be used to protect a name or symbol, but, generally speaking, the person proving first use will receive registration for the name.

The ® indicates that the trademark is registered with the Patent and Trademark office in Washington, D.C. No one else can use this name.

Do not use a circle R, ®, unless the product has a federal trademark registration. You will see other marks, such as "s.m." This is a service mark, most often used for protecting slogans or a catchy advertising line. Tag lines on commercials or in advertisements are most often protected with an "s.m." at their end.

Fortunes have been lost by companies who have not protected their brand names. A problem you will face is that some companies don't have well-defined policies for trademark protection. This is because they haven't had any problems. Yet.

I had a client introduce a new type of computer product at a time when there must have been 100 new computer products introduced every day across the country. Everyone was naming their systems high-tech sounding names, usually including the words "tech," "data," "sonic," "micro," "macro," "mini," "electro" or something similarly redundant.

Naturally, companies at one end of the country were coming up with the same names as companies at the other.

My client spent six months promoting a new product under a completely original name—we thought. After thousands of dollars were spent in brochures, photography, video tapes, and other marketing, a letter arrived.

A competitor could prove they had been using the same name on a similar product for a longer period of time. This may have meant only a six-month difference in use, but the earlier company had correctly protected the name with the trademark symbol and could prove that they had aggressively kept others from using it.

My client had to rename the product and redo all the materials in the next couple of months. This was a very expensive mistake to make.

You can help your client by asking how they protect their trademarks and copyrights. If they don't have a program for doing this, you can further help them and yourself by suggesting a formal guide to their protected names. This guide instructs salespeople, customers, and the general public about the proper use of the trade-market name.

Here's another writing project you can sell to your client. You can write this guide. Many companies already have these and will send you theirs free for the asking. Write and request a trademark guide from various corporations and use them as examples for the trademark guide you write for your client.

Gender Considerations

The English language was designed in a way that defaults to the masculine when there is any question whether we're referring to a man or woman.

I distinctly remember the day in elementary school when the teacher told us about this. She explained that when we used "he" in a sentence, it could mean either "he" or "she."

Our entire class accepted this and went along defaulting to "he" when conversation demanded it.

Then came the 60's, and the world was turned upside-down. Everyone's role changed. What we had taken for granted as correct in many of our attitudes turned out to be wrong. Or at least inappropriate. At least temporarily.

The social revolution changed the attention given all groups of people. One of these was women. This put writers in a bind because existing language couldn't cope with it easily.

You see, everyone didn't have Mrs. Miller at the Campus Lab Elementary school. Some people had her but missed the day when she explained that "he" meant both sexes. What do we do in business writing?

Business writing is usually best served with the use of neutral gender.

This is good and bad.

The intent is good because it makes it more obvious that women are included. When writing isn't in neutral gender, the tendency is to use a "he/she" or a "he or she" in the writing.

I'm so glad this system of he/sheisms has largely disappeared. It is awkward and clumsy. Worse, it makes for terribly self-conscious writing. Sentences are impossible to read with the "he or she" ganged together in them.

To make writing gender-neutral, use the third person plural. By writing "they, their and them" you can get yourself out of most of the grammar traps that neutral-speak presents. Just be sure all references within the sentence are plural, for consistency.

Along the same lines, when you write about job titles, you may be used to writing "salesmen and saleswomen" or "salesmen/women." The easy way out is to add the word "person" to gender-neutralize the work. This is fine. "Salesperson" has a nice ring to it. But what you write will read better if you can more specifically title the job.

For example, a "salesperson" might be a "sales rep," or a "sales representative." And while the job we used to call "fireman" isn't quite right when we call it "fireperson," "fire fighter" fits both men and women who put out fires. Fire fighter is also more descriptive and gives some indication of the work that person does.

Look for a descriptive name for the job title. You can invent titles and use them too.

In writing this book, I've tried to present the material in a neutral fashion. Where a he or she seemed appropriate to the story, or couldn't be helped, I used it. A generation from now we will have sorted this whole thing out. New words and grammar rules will be established and used in a way that won't cause concern or disrupt the flow of the language. Until then, be sensitive to the issue, use your best judgment, and work with words inventively.

Chapter 6

Prospecting for Clients

"Someone Will Hire ME To Write?"

"Who's going to hire me?" you may wonder.

"Come on, you're a great writer. I've never known anyone who could take a bunch of complicated information and organize it like you. You're straightforward in your presentation, and you've got a nice light touch," a colleague insists.

"Yeh, but how're they going to know I exist. Maybe I could stand outside their headquarters and throw rocks up at the windows," you jest.

"I think the phone would be better."

"Throw the phone at the windows?"

"No, get on the phone and talk to them, it's just a matter of learning how to do it."

Call, Don't Write

It's possible to find clients with a small direct mail program. A simple cover letter outlining your skills with a business card enclosed may get you some response, though cost is a big item in direct mail. You have to pay for printing and postage, and you have to develop a mailing list. All of this is costly, time-consuming, and difficult to follow up.

While referrals are the number-one way to get new clients, cold calls on the telephone are the next best thing.

The method that has consistently produced the best results is the telephone.

The telephone can get you into practically every office in any company. People will stop to take a phone call under nearly any circumstance. For some reason, our society has created such an aura around the phone that its ring demands an immediate response. A person on the other end of the phone line requires immediate and complete attention, while the person sitting with someone in an office does not.

Even a written phone message tells people something is happening and they'd better find out what they missed. Damn the people waiting to see them in person.

So the best rule when contacting clients is don't write them. Call. Don't send a resume, don't even keep one. Don't send a sample. Instead, take your work to them, discuss what you do, evaluate their needs, and show how you can fill them.

This may sound preachy and pushy, but too many freelancers slow themselves down while trying to get started. When you're trying to sell marketing or communications, use a straightforward approach. Use the skills you're trying to sell the potential client.

One of the worst things you can do is send a cute letter. One of the biggest complaints I've heard about freelance writers trying to crack into a corporation is about letters that waste a potential client's time.

This is an example of the beginning of a poorly written letter that was sent to a corporate client:

Dear Decision Maker,

Why do you need an alert, fresh talent performing corporate writing duties for you? Because my writing skills are what you need to convey the important messages about your products and services to customers.

It hit the trash can fast.

First, the client doesn't have time to read letters. If they're going to hire you, they will pick up the phone and get you into their office. Corporate communications move fast. Decisions to send out assignments are made in the morning, and the freelance writer is often in that same afternoon to get work underway.

Second, you're addressing a pro in your letter. Know the name of the person you're trying to get in touch with. Explain what you do and your availability.

Third, don't write a letter at all, unless they ask for it. Use the phone to get into the office and locate the person who can give you assignments.

If you want clients, you can get more of them faster by using the telephone. Letters will never be answered.

When to Call

When do you call?

Early in the morning is usually the best time to get people in a corporation. Try the minute they walk in the door. Start at 7 AM, which is actually before most people are at work. When you don't get through, try 7:30, then 8:00.

Any time in the morning up to 11:30 is prime telephone time for cold calling. After 11:30 is lunch time and people are usually out. How long they're gone varies with the part of the country and the type of business. Some companies provide a cafeteria with free lunch. They do this to keep the employees from wandering out to eat and spending company time doing it. So your potential client is probably at the cafeteria chowing down if you call during lunch.

People tend to check back at their desks for messages before heading off to lunch and right after they get back from eating. Afternoons are often slow. Right after lunch most corporate employees would be better off taking a nap than trying to get back into the swing of things. The Italians figured this out and let their entire country shut down every afternoon.

While morning is typically the best time to call, you can score an assignment any time of the day. Try between three and five PM. By this time your potential client has been through a tough day and realizes what a help a good freelance writer could be in getting some work done. Experimenting with calling times will help you determine what's most successful for you.

From my experience, the best days to call and prospect for new clients are Tuesday, Wednesday, and Thursday. In that order. Mondays are OK, but at the beginning of the week there isn't the same mind-set in a corporation. On Mondays, you're dealing with private citizens who spent the weekend sleeping in and lounging around the house. They haven't been energized by the corporate environment yet.

Fridays are useless. Anything that happens in a business after 10 o'clock on a Friday is vaporized out of your client's mind by the time they leave the building that afternoon. If you call Friday, the potential client has forgotten you totally by Monday morning. Friday's also the day when everyone leaves early. Friday is the day the gang gets together for drinks after work to hash things over.

Concentrate on Tuesdays and Wednesdays for the most attentive prospective client, but break that rule and call when you intuitively feel the time is right, too.

Reaching the Person Who Can Hire You

How do you reach potential clients to let them know you're out there ready to write and have them pay you to do it? Most importantly, how do you find the specific people within their organization who need a freelance writer?

Don't make it hard on yourself. It's easy to find out exactly who can hire you at your target company. Just call and ask. This is where your business writing client list can begin to grow. It is also where you can let it become more trouble than you think it's worth and give up.

Begin by picking up the phone. Call into the prospect company and ask for marketing. There may be more than one marketing organization. There might be one for each product or service that the company sells. If they ask which marketing department, use your knowledge of their products. Ask for the marketing director for their most popular product. Tell the receptionist you'd like to talk with the "marketing director for _____" and name the product they currently have that is the most successful—and making them the most money.

More generally, you can ask for corporate sales, corporate communications, or advertising. Then ask for the person who hires freelance writers. Don't make it any more complicated than that.

Say, "Who hires freelance writers?" This will put you through, we hope, to the person who has the biggest marketing and advertising budget. He or she will also be the busiest person in the company. Or at least it will seem that way.

Your chances of getting this individual on the phone right away are fair. But you're likely to be shunted off to someone else, too. This is all right. Begin with someone in the right general area of the company. Don't start complicating the situation with a grand explanation of your talents. Instead, talk to the person conversationally, asking questions to learn more about their company. Know what they do in advance so that you know what products they're talking about. Gradually, ask for names of individuals who work with freelance writers.

Frequently the first couple of people you talk to don't know who does this. They may not have any knowledge about people in our line of work, or who within their own organization is the best for you to talk to. Get them to refer you to their boss. Or ask for a couple of other logical people who can help you with your search.

In any telephone contact, be ready to talk with a receptionist or secretary. They run interference for their bosses. Also help the people you get on the phone to understand what you want, since they may have no idea what to do with your call.

In every case, and whenever this opportunity presents itself, ask the name of the head of their marketing department. And ask to speak with that person. Eventually you will work you way up—or down—the organization and reach the decision-maker, the person in the company with the budget and inclination to hire a freelance writer.

Breaking Through The Runaround

If you make repeated calls and get nowhere, use the opportunity to tell the secretary whom you've talked to several times and that you've called all over the company. Say that you can't understand why you've been told repeatedly that the head of the marketing department (for example) was the person to talk to. Make sure to mention the name of that person when referring to him or her. This adds credibility.

Be certain to ask the name of everyone you talk to along the way. This removes the facelessness the telephone gives people. Knowing their name forces them to treat you as an individual and to be responsible for what they tell you.

When referred to another person, say "Ms. Smith suggested I talk with you, Mr. Brown." This moves you miles ahead in the process, by creating a sense of familiarity with their organization. It makes you an instant insider. Remembering names—writing them down—and using them, increases your visibility. It will get you through to people who would be otherwise inaccessible.

Don't give up. Phoning into a company and finding the person you need to talk to can take days—even weeks. Keep notes on the process you go through. Write down names, phone numbers, and who referred you from one person to another. Create a file on each company if you need to in order to track your exploration better.

Once You Find the Right Person

Many freelancers fall apart once their prospecting leads them to the right person. When they find the person who can actually assign them writing projects, they blow the whole thing.

A classic example of this is a writer telling a potential client how inexperienced he is.

"I'm new at this and am not sure if I can do it, but I'd like to try."

Another thing an insecure beginning freelance writer will do is ask for on-the-job training.

"Hire me cheap, I'll learn how to do this writing, really."

No one wants to pay for your training.

On the phone you can come across as confident, as powerful and as sure of yourself as you dare. Even if you're doing the dishes with the phone on your shoulder. Even if it takes you a week to write a 50-word radio spot, you can still sound authoritative.

Think through your first telephone contact with the right person. What are you going to say?

Begin by introducing yourself. Say, "This is Betty Morrison calling."

Don't say, "Hello, how are you today?" You don't care how the person is and they don't care how you are. Your asking an inane question of someone you don't know tips them off that some outsider is trying to act familiar with them.

Also don't say, "Hello, my name is Betty Morrison." That's like describing yourself to somebody. You know who you are and what you are, so say your name. Your name is you.

Say, "This is Betty Morrison." It's simple and direct. There is a subtle difference. You are announcing that you are somebody. Follow up with the straight facts. "I'm a freelance writer based in the Twin Cities and I'd like to find out about writing opportunities in Acme Company."

Here, in a couple of sentences, you've made your case. If this is the person you should be talking to, you're ready to get down to business. If you still haven't reached the right person, ask who you should be talking to.

Even if it's the right contact, the chances you'll immediately get an assignment are still slim. You're more likely to hear, "We don't have any work for freelance writers now."

If you do, reply by saying, "Good, then this is the perfect time for me to come in and introduce myself to you and find out what sorts of future writing needs you might have."

Don't give them the opportunity to reject you. Every obstacle presented is an opportunity for you. What you want now is a face-to-face appointment. Say, "I'd like to introduce myself to you. When could I come by?"

Be this simple and direct. People in business always feel they are in a time crunch, whether they actually are or not. By talking this positive approach, you come across as knowing what you want, and you will immediately begin to develop their confidence. Then you can get to what they want in the way of writing skills.

Practice using the telephone. It can get you into any office anywhere. The phone will solve problems for you, help you make contacts and get your bills paid.

Use the same method to follow up a referral when someone refers you to a potential client. Call up the person, tell the name of the individual who suggested you call, and let him or her decide what to do with you.

Don't be afraid of rejection. You'll get many noes for every yes. And don't keep hounding the same people all the time. The best estimate for a successful call ratio is that one assignment comes from about every ten cold calls.

If assignments are not forthcoming from a potential client, call the contact occasionally—every four weeks or so. And make sure the list of people you're following up on is long, never less than 30. This way you spread out your self-promotion and have a better chance of getting the assignment you want.

A more complete suggestion for a telephone contact follows.

Sample Prospecting Phone Call

WRITER: This is Betty Morrison. I've been freelance writing based out of the Twin Cities for 5 years. I understand you work with freelancers, and I wanted to introduce myself to you.

PROSPECT: Oh, we occasionally hire writers, but there's nothing going on now. Why don't you check back in a couple months.

WRITER: If there aren't any assignments now, this is a perfect time to get in touch. I'd like you to know my capabilities, so when something comes up you can give me a call.

PROSPECT: Send me a resume and some samples then.

WRITER: I don't have a resume. Resumes are for people looking for jobs, and you see, I freelance. I don't intend to look for a job. I prefer to freelance full time. And there's no way I'd have enough samples of my work to send out every time someone asked for them. I've tried sending samples, but I just don't get them back. However, I'd be glad to show you my portfolio if we could set up a time to go over it.

PROSPECT: I really don't have the time. I'm up to my eye-balls-in-alligators for the next three weeks.

WRITER: Well, I feel that successful freelance writing requires a good, solid relationship between the writer and client. I've made it a rule to get to know clients before a project, so that we understand each other. If you'd like to have another freelance writer available as a resource, it'll only take 10 minutes to go over my work. I figure that if people aren't going to take the time for that when there isn't the pressure of a project, we probably won't be able to work well together when it really comes to the crunch.

PROSPECT: You're right.

WRITER: How does next week look?

PROSPECT: I can't meet at all on Tuesday.

WRITER: What about Wednesday afternoon? I'm free at three.

PROSPECT: OK. See you then.

WRITER: Is there anyone else in your company who works with freelance writers that I should see at the same time?

PROSPECT: Yes, there's Jayme Cameron. I'll ask her to meet with us.

WRITER: Thank you. See you at three on Wednesday the twenty-fifth.

There are a thousand variations on a good phone call. Use this as a model and adapt it to a successful format that you're comfortable with.

Market Yourself Along with Your Skills

It doesn't pay to be bashful with potential clients. You must promote yourself mercilessly. Find out who has the power and the budget within a company. Then ask them for assignments. Don't be at all shy when doing this.

You'll only get what you want if you ask for it. Speak frankly to people. "Why don't you hire me?" "Why didn't I get that assignment? It was right up my alley." When you hear about something you missed, make it clear you know that an assignment was given and that you didn't get it. Find out why and try to correct the situation for next time.

It is always to your best advantage to develop a straightforward relationship with a client. When you do, work will seem to appear from nowhere. Sometimes there is budget money set aside to employ a writer and it goes unused because no one knows the right freelance writer to hire. If they know you, you'll get the call. If you notice that something needs to be done for a company—something as obvious as a brochure providing a general summary of a company's activities—find the right person and suggest it. And make sure they understand that you're the person to do the writing on it.

Use your creative mind on the corporation. Loosen them up and get them thinking about things in new ways. By suggesting assignments and directions for their business, you get more work and become a valuable asset to the client.

You can subtly separate yourself from the ordinary corporate employee in ways that make you interesting to them and get you invited back. Tell them about your life, about things that are out of the norm. Give them something interesting to get the conversation off business issues when you can.

One successful freelance business writer prided himself on having a new, upbeat story to tell his clients whenever he came in. He swore it wasn't his writing that got him repeat business, it was the tall tales about fishing, trips to the mountains, his lobbying for environmental causes, and visits to foreign cities.

The same guy thought that refusing to wear a tie helped set him apart, too. Ties are a touchy issue. Ridiculous, too. Whether a man wears a piece of cloth tied around his neck can greatly affect his success in a corporation.

It is interesting that the tie was first adopted by the French from Croation mercenaries during the Thirty Years War. From these arbitrary beginnings it became an irrevocable convention. So wear a neck tie when you need to. There is plenty of time to sit around at home in your underwear working while everyone else is in business suits at their offices. When trying to stand apart from the others in a corporate environment, choose less obvious ways to do it. It's absurd how this can make a difference, but you can probably loosen up your personal dress code once your clients get to know you.

Writing for Big Accounts

Your first big account can be joyful and exciting. To be suddenly plucked off the pavement and thrust into the fast pace of a business communications program is exhilarating.

This happened to me early in my freelance career. Like most freelance writing assignments, it didn't happen in a logical manner. Through an odd connection I developed a major client that lasted three years.

It began with a call from a very small audio-visual producer. This was a two-man outfit that felt it needed a writer to help it pace its work more effectively. They figured a writer was an inexpensive way to give them more time to produce current projects while freeing them up to look for new ones.

This A.V. firm had an assignment to produce a series of slide shows with an energetic client. The client was riding the crest of an electronics revolution and couldn't seem to expand fast enough. The A.V. producer took me along to their first meeting. At this meeting, the client company's marketing manager met me and offered the writing assignments for the printed materials he was planning to produce.

It wasn't long before I told the small A.V. firm they really didn't need a writer. They really needed a director-producer to give them more time to allow them to prosper. We agreed that I would continue my relationship with the client company and I quietly bowed out as their A.V. writer.

At the same time, the work I was doing directly for the client—which was all print—got so big I could barely keep up with it. There was one project after another, all coming from the head of one division. I got along with him well, put up with a bundle of eccentric habits, and managed to last longer than any other vendor he had used. He went through printers, photo separators, designers, messenger services, typesetters, translators, and keyliners—one right after another. Each wasn't called back because of some perceived shortcoming in his work. For three years I could get the client on the phone when nobody else could. He'd always have new assignments ready to go.

Eventually he moved to another company. I thought I was done with this major account and would have to go looking for another to replace it. Meanwhile I continued to develop new clients.

When the new marketing manager came on board, I was surprised when he called me in. He asked me to come over immediately for a meeting, and I was to bring my portfolio. Based on our brief introductory meeting, he hired me for three major projects.

I was pleased at this, but didn't want to work exclusively for one client. I knew I needed to get consistent assignments from several companies, rather than have my income so dependent on just one. I was pleased with myself for continuing to seek assignments elsewhere because my relationship with this new manager didn't work out. It wasn't long before I voluntarily decided to stop working for him. this was none too soon since he began having problems with other vendors too.

It's often tough to stay with a client when your contact person changes jobs. It's good to try to do it, but realize that it won't work unless it's a comfortable transition. The new person should want you to stay and should be someone you work with easily or the relationship will not last.

Retail Business Writing—Pros and Cons

There are all types of businesses and all sizes of companies. Each has its own communication needs. some are trying to sell something, either a product or service. They may also need writing that communicates with their employees, instructs, tells their story to the public or a thousand other things.

However, when you first consider freelance writing for business, your immediate impulse will be to head for the retailers who constantly run ads in the newspapers. It looks like they have tons of money to spend and your skills would fit right in. Advertising copy looks easy to write, and everybody gets to see your work. Three-fourths of any Sunday paper is ads—right?

As obvious a source of income and intoxicating as it looks from the outside—if you have one retail client to write for, that will likely be more than enough. Retail businesses will eat up your time and tend to pay you less for your writing.

The experiences you have with a retail client might be much different. You may have good luck with them.

However, the negative characteristics can be:
• Too little time between assignments
• Constant and last minute changes
• Pressure to keep pumping out new advertising
• Personality conflicts developing very quickly

There are exceptions to this:
• A good retail client can nicely compliment your other clients by adding diversity.
• There is satisfaction in opening the Sunday newspaper to see an ad you wrote.

Often you can negotiate a trade out with your retail client. If your client is a stereo store, you could probably trade your time for equipment at a prearranged discount. If you do this, be certain to make the arrangement in advance. Put the details in writing. At the end of each month, or the end of each project, invoice the company for a cash amount. On the invoice, note that this amount will be traded out for merchandise and state the percentage of the discount.

Trade outs like this are taxable as income. Keep complete records, and if you have any questions, talk it over with your accountant.

The big retailers in your area probably have their corporate headquarters somewhere else. The advertising is written far away and placed in your local newspaper from a distance.

If there are good-size local (not chain) department stores, shopping centers, and other retail businesses, they probably do their advertising in-house or use an agency.

If they use an advertising agency, they're probably one of that agency's major accounts, so the agency will protect it and do the work themselves—although it will be handled by junior staff members. If the advertising is done in-house, it's probably considered a starter job for a college student.

On the upbeat side, retailing is an entrance into advertising work for many writers. It's easy to pick up, and it isn't complicated work.

If you want to write for a retail business, a fairly modest-size retail account is your best bet. Look for a medium-size business that sells something you're interested in. Imported furniture, if that's your interest, or a clothing store, if you're into clothes. Select this retail client carefully, using a lot of intuition. You want their style of selling to match yours. If they are aggressive, that better be your style too. They should be conservative if you're conservative, or full of pizzazz if you possess that elusive quality. When they say that they're selling quality merchandise, you'd better feel that it's quality too.

Walk into their store and notice what it feels like to you. Are people in there enjoying themselves? Do the customers feel good about buying products there? What feeling do you pick up from the place?

Retail ad writing is a time-consuming business. When the business is privately owned, all the decisions will be made by one person. This can mean you face an individual who has one way of doing something and it'll never change. Worse, the decisions can be made by an entire family, with every member having a note and a different opinion. It can also mean that the group of owners don't know what consistency in advertising is. They may not realize a style should be established in their ads and that they must bring themselves to develop a cohesive marketing plan and stick to it.

Chapter 7

Once You Get Started

Avoiding Time-Wasters

Prospecting is important to your success. But it's just as important to avoid wasting your precious time at it. Learn ways to maximize your return. Here's an example of the type of time-waster you might encounter.

A company selling a specific type of medical insurance had a marketing director who was young and aggressive. This fellow was very full of himself because he perceived his job as extremely important and prestigious. He had been suddenly plucked from a dullish corporate position and elevated to this rapidly growing company. Here he had money to spend and many ways to push himself along in the business world's fast lane.

My first encounter with him seemed promising. I was called in by an audio-visual production company to write a proposal for a script. The young executive kept us waiting in the lobby for half an hour for no particular reason. Eventually, we were ushered in. The producer, director and I—as writer—took time to come to his office to consider the assignment of a video-taped program. We met for an hour.

During this meeting we seemed to establish good rapport. The client-to-be told me how he liked working with writers, and the producer and director felt we got along well. We went on to talk about developing a treatment and really got down to specifics on it.

Everything seemed just great, and the job looked like it would happen and happen fast. All we needed to have was another meeting to confirm the outline and all the details.

In the week after the meeting, I put in a couple more hours writing a treatment of the show. And I spent more time meeting with the video production company to make sure it would be producible within the budget they were proposing.

Another meeting was scheduled and the three of us trooped down to the young executive's company to present it. The man kept us waiting again, then let us in to his office for a brief visit. We presented the treatment I had written, and during this exchange he seemed a little more distracted, and he hurried through it. Afterwards he said thanks and he'd let us know if we would be selected to produce the program.

A week later the producer followed up with a phone call. The busy client said he wasn't going to produce the show at all, but thanks anyway. By chance, a few days later another audio-visual producer told me he had been assigned the project. He had even received the assignment before our second meeting with the client.

The youngish corporate flake had wasted our time. Because he couldn't make a decision about who to hire, or was on a power trip, he thought he could call people in at any time he pleased—without concern for their time. He hauled writers and other vendors in and put them through their paces whenever he felt like it.

When I told my producer and director that he had given the assignment to someone else before we'd made our presentation—they only said that they'd mention this to him if he called them asking for another proposal sometime. They didn't want to confront him for fear he'd be angry and never consider them for another assignment.

A year later I ran into the corporate flake at the meeting of a civic volunteer organization. In front of a circle of his "peers," I told a story about the hardships of freelance writing, specifically about an anonymous company, one that sounded a lot like his, who had me, a producer and director, waste time in a proposal session on an already assigned project. As I told the story, I didn't name the company or people involved.

The guy didn't exactly acknowledge that he recognized himself in the story. However, he excused himself quickly from the conversation.

He knew he'd made a big mistake and would certainly think twice before doing it again. I hope taking the chance of pointing it out to him in this gentle way saved another writer grief sometime in the future.

Should you take the same risk in confronting a potential client, who has wasted your time and not been honest with you?

Maybe.

It depends on what they did and how carefully you can let them know you're onto their act.

So, did I ever work for that time-waster of his company?

No, I haven't yet. But I really don't think my chances have been hurt. And should the situation arise, I'd feel very comfortable in a meeting with him.

Educating Your Clients

People only buy a couple of houses in a lifetime. They buy more cars than that on the average. But groceries are something they select and buy every week. The things people are most familiar with are the things they can judge the quality of and most accurately determine what should be paid for them.

Buying writing is a foreign experience for most people. So is the process that involves creating a piece of writing that is acceptable to them. This is usually complicated by the fact that your clients typically don't know what they want. Consequently they won't be good at determining an appropriate fee for your writing.

To get the most out of your relationship with a client, you will probably have to train them. This means educating them about the complexities of the writing process and getting them to realize what your skills are worth.

If you're meeting with a client for the first time and aren't certain what to expect, be careful. You can protect yourself from a bad start in several ways.

• Check the client out before you arrange a meeting and during the first encounter, ask if they've worked with a freelance writer before. If they haven't, tell them about the way you like to work. They could be new to this and need to have the process detailed.

• Explain in detail how many drafts of the material you expect to write before an final draft is accepted. See that there is enough time to accomplish the necessary revisions before the deadline.

• Tell them what you will charge for the project. Usually charging on a project basis is the best method. Clients are anxious to know how much something is going to cost. Too often going by an hourly charge makes the writing impossibly expensive. For example, I currently quote $100 per hour. At this time, that is as high as you can comfortably go with an hourly quote in my market. Every town is different. Location, cost of living, competition and other factors dictate what you can get. What's important is know what your market will bear. Find out what others are charging and use it as a guide. Hit the middle of the range as you're getting started.

• If you have the slightest suspicion that there will be trouble getting paid, ask if they will pay you within 10 days of invoice and if you can have a purchase order number.

• It's a good idea to send a new client a letter after a first meeting, spelling out the terms of the assignment, including the amount you will charge and how soon after invoicing you will receive your check. If you're really queasy about their paying, or have heard of other vendors having trouble, ask for half of the fee when you start the project and the second half when you finish.

• First meetings set the tone for the project and the relationship. The main thrust of your meeting must be the project, getting the essential information about the subject, setting a schedule, and arranging to turn in quality work on time.

I'm told by clients that the strongest impressions they get of freelance writers are in the way they handle the first meeting. If they see the writer is alert and interested, a good base has been established. If the client senses that you understood the substance of the information and the tone they wished it to take that first meeting, they'll approach your first draft with the assumption that it'll be good.

• Take careful notes. Repeat important points back to be sure you have interpreted them correctly.

• Ask good questions to get at their motivations. I've found that the best questions to ask are the ones I already know the answers to. These let you compare what you think you understand to what the client is really trying to get across.

Some writers record meetings on a cassette player, particularly first meetings. This lets the client know you're getting all the information correctly. A tape recording of the criteria that are set at the start can provide ample evidence later if your client changes a project in some way that throws you off or adds to the work you're required to do. It's also a refresher if you missed a detail here or there.

I've never felt I needed a recorder. It seemed like something else to break down at the wrong time. Also, I never thought I had the patience to go back and listen to a meeting again—most of them are hard enough to sit through the first time.

Another reason I don't use a recorder is I hate the sound of my own voice—and I'm afraid I'd feel I wasn't listening during the meeting as closely if I knew a recorder was preserving my every word. Experiment with a friend's recorder first, to see if you like it, before making the investment.

First meetings can color your whole relationship with a client. Get a good start by making your first contact a very positive, professional experience for both of you.

People will often call you with an assignment when they know nothing more than they "need something written." What they really require is someone from the outside, who is not so caught up in their business to determine what they're really trying to say, to whom it needs to be said, and what form it should take.

Many clients don't realize that rewriting is essential to successful writing. In fact it usually takes a first draft just to get them thinking clearly about the topic you're writing on.

"You missed the point," they'll say, or, "You're way off target, I can't believe you don't understand what we were talking about here." The problem is that they didn't know what they wanted in the first place. It takes a first draft to get them thinking cohesively. Their thoughts were just floating around in the air and now they see them for the first time on paper.

Take time to walk your client through the entire business writing process before you begin the research. Even if they are experienced, the first time you work with them let them know what you're going to do.

Begin by telling them that you'll research the subject and get the information you need for an outline. This means talking to everyone they recommend as part of the information-gathering process.

Depending on the project, you might suggest you have another meeting after the research phase to review an outline of the material. This is extremely important, as it clarifies the direction of the project. It also helps the client focus on what they really want to get across before you have expended a lot of time on an approach they may not agree with. When they concur that your outline is on target, explain that you will deliver a first draft. If you are comfortable with the client's ability to digest what you've written, tell them you will leave it for their review. More often than not when you leave the material they don't get around to reading it until your next meeting anyway.

Label this draft of the copy either a "first draft" or a "rough draft." The label "rough draft" is best if the client is insecure with the writing process and doesn't understand the importance of rewriting. Too often you'll find they consider what you turn in initially is all you're going to do—rather than a starting point for refining the material.

Make sure they understand that writing is a fluid process that takes cooperation by both of you. Establish the fact that you're going to work at getting along, listening to what they want, and will rewrite the copy to satisfy their needs. And that this may require several drafts.

You'll find that by sharing your experiences with a client and making it clear that they understand the way you work, your business writing projects will go more smoothly. And they will be approved faster. You'll spend less time while getting paid more.

Keeping Your Client on Track

One thing you don't want to do is make a reliable client's work harder, or help that person get himself fired. Freelance writers can come up with inappropriate ideas and actions that cause clients big problems.

Most people you work for—like their companies—are quite conservative in their approach to communications. They are overly afraid of doing something wrong. They'd rather be safe, secure, and boring than trust their own inventiveness.

This is where you come in. You are the writer—the person they can bounce ideas off and get a bunch of ideas back to choose from. When ideas are presented at a committee meeting, you'll probably come up with more than anyone else.

When kicking around ideas, remind your clients that all the ideas you come up with won't work. The reason you're mentioning so many is to act as a creative catalyst for the group.

Beware. It's easy to get carried away. When there's a flash of inspiration about a project and it's hot, anything can happen. Getting carried away with ideas can happen with all types of projects. Press releases can overemphasize a strange theme. It sounds like a good "hook" when you first think of it, but once it's out in the real world and not in the cozy secure, corporate office environment, it doesn't make any sense.

The simplest, but not the best, test of an idea is to circulate it with the people at the company where you are writing the project. Company people often don't have much perspective on their products because they work with them every day. They're more likely to react to the personality of the person presenting the idea than to the content and the context in which it will be presented when in final form.

If you have the time, it's better to take the idea home and present it to friends. Think about it yourself. Trust your own feelings about it. If you're uncomfortable with a theme, product name, or approach to an assignment, and you're having problems working it out, tell the client. Figure out what's clumsy about it and what new direction you can take that will be better.

Save your client. It's easy to run away with an idea if there is a big budget. When a lot of money is going to be spent, everyone gets excited. They become less worried that it is spent well and more concerned about being one of the people who gets to do the spending—or in seeing that some of it gets spent on them, their product or their division.

Combine a runaway idea that wasn't properly thought out with an intoxicatingly big budget, and a disaster may not be far off.

The worst runaway idea I saw was when an advertising communications company was given a big account for producing motivational films. Their client was a big processed-food manufacturer. This company was in tight competition with a competitor who sold a nearly identical product. They wanted to punch up sales. It was critical that their slipping market share be saved.

The local communications company was given a huge budget to produce an audio-visual program for a major sales conference. They had handled big budget projects for this client and knew that if they produced a good A.V. project, they could continue to make thousands of dollars profit from the client.

To handle this project, the client sent in their liaison person from headquarters. He worked with advertising communications for the company and knew the film had to be a success. There wasn't much time. Days passed quickly. The film was scripted and went into production. It was a long, hard shoot. Very expensive, too. But the film makers were pleased with the results.

At last it was time to preview the program. The film was complete and a big premier ready. With all the upper management in the room, the liaison person from the company and the director, writer, and producer of the film anxiously waited for a positive reaction.

The lights dimmed and the show began. This is what their big budget and untamed ideas produced:

The show opened with an Olympic torch bearer. It had been an Olympic year, and a great deal of attention had focused on the games. It seemed a good tie-in. Holding the Olympic torch high in the air, the symbol of international brotherhood and understanding, an athlete-actor ran around a stadium track. A stern expression of competition and conditioning tightened on his face.

He rounded the last corner of the track and headed up the stairs as the audio track played the sounds of a cheering crowd and Olympicesque music. Up the steps he climbed, faster and faster, toward the highest part of the stadium. The spirit of the Olympic games was captured in the expensive footage that would open the client's major sales conference of the year.

At the top of the stadium, the Olympic runner reached a great dish. Paused. A cheer went up from the throng below.

Slowly, he reached the flame into the dish's center.

The camera pulled back to show a major competitor's taste test display standing in the dish. The athlete ignited the display stand with the torch of Olympic understanding.

The competition's symbol burst into flames as the crowd roared.

The production was very expensive. And entirely inappropriate. To use the Olympic symbols so inappropriately was stupidity at its highest. It's an example of how self involved people can become when a project gets going fast and no steadying influence steps in.

The production company was fired. The revenues lost from that client exceeded several hundred thousand dollars a year. The client's liaison person was let go for the gaff and there were rumors of other people's jobs being shuffled around in the client's marketing department for weeks afterwards.

Yes, gross and costly mistakes happen even when the highest levels of corporations use skilled vendors. They happen just as easily there as they do in small companies for the same reasons.

There are situations where a freelance writer can step in and say, "Excuse me, but I think this is inappropriate. Why don't we try something a little less violent and ostentatious or crude? How about something a little more creative? Such as . . ."

Benefiting From Company Transition Periods

Many times you will hear this from a potential client:

"We're going through budget cuts." Or, "They've just let half the people in this department go." How about—"I'm doing the work of three people now, I just don't know how to get all of it done."

You can read the newspapers to hear what's happening to businesses in your area. They are forever expanding and contracting. This happens when sales projections aren't met. A new vice president is named and 30 people lose their jobs, or 50 are hired for a new project.

Sometimes you call into a company you'd like to work for and it sounds like you're being asked to enroll in a kid's tree house club. A new marketing manager has just arrived and is drawing together a group of dedicated followers. There are vendors who are expected to do whatever the manager wishes. All this person wants in return for assignments is complete loyalty. There isn't an open, professional approach. It's all chummy and closed in. You don't need this. Go work for somebody else if you aren't treated professionally.

At times, companies reduce their staff sizes. They let people go because salaries are a major expense and a quick way to balance budgets. You'd think this would be a terrible time to approach them for work. Actually, a transition in a company can be good. Work still needs to be done, and they're apt to go to an outside writer because they don't have authorization to hire anyone full time. And they can't write themselves.

The same is true when people change jobs. A new manager in marketing, advertising, or public relations is a perfect candidate for a phone call from you. A new person is usually looking for good resources to draw from. Someone new to a position is anxious for fresh people, so they're not shackled to the same old ideas or loyalties. If you hear about personnel changes, get in touch with the company. When there are moves in a corporation, or when they tell you they're going through budget cuts, stay on them. Changes and hard times mean a company is taking another look at itself and wants to try something new. After all, if the old ways of doing things worked, they wouldn't have had to make the changes.

Every change in a corporation is an opportunity for a freelance writer.

Anchor Clients

Whether you plan it this way or not, your work load will probably consist of one, two, or three major clients. Some will have a lot of work for you and others a little. Whatever the work load, they will be a reliable source of work. These are anchor clients.

Getting good anchor clients takes time, so once you get them, hang on to them.

A solid client can smooth out your writing income. With the promise of one or two good strong accounts, many writers have left full-time jobs and moved into freelancing. They have followed up leads and developed relationships with individuals in companies they realized could be steady clients they could count on for a substantial amount of work. Once on their own, these writers continued to market their skills, gradually increasing their client contacts and making their business grow.

Wherever you are starting from, your freelance business writing will probably develop the same pattern: your anchor clients will take up most of your time, with other writing assignments filling in.

Once established with an account, you should be able to call the client and ask for an assignment. They will also let you know about work that is coming up in advance and you'll be able to count on the income.

There are other benefits to having good anchor clients. If you need proof of income when applying for a loan, you can have the bank contact your client for assurance that there is a substantial amount of work for you coming up in the future.

Anchor clients will change. Three years often seems to be an average stay with any one major account. Changes happen when people are promoted, the products or services you are helping them sell are phased out, or you outgrow them.

Always be looking to the future. Keep watch for new clients of every type and size. Any one of them—even the smallest and least obvious—can become an important source of work.

Losing Your Contact Person at a Company

If you hit it off with a client, it can be a long and happy relationship. You can feel secure in the promise of continued work and professional growth. That's a blessed but rare commodity.

When your client leaves, it is typical to have a new set of vendors take over the work when the new person takes your client's place. On the bright side, your established client obviously thought you were good and actually may be going to a better position in another company. With luck, your old client may take you along to that new company.

Screening Clients

Finding new clients looks tough at first. After you've had enough practice at it, you'll develop a routine that will feel comfortable. Eventually you'll have a list of clients you can count on for work. And you will be able to select clients you like to work for, rather than taking every assignment that comes along, just to get by.

It'll take some time before you feel secure enough to drop a client, but at some point you will be selecting clients as a matter of course. You'll be able to tell what it is about them that fits with your style and what doesn't.

Writing is a specialized business. It is a very personal service you perform while working closely with a client.

So, how can you get the attention of the right people in the businesses that need your writing services?

Almost any approach you take can help you get writing assignments of some kind. Some methods just work better than others.

Placing ads about yourself in local general or business publications will probably go unnoticed. It is extremely difficult to present your best qualities in the pages of a regional business journal, for example, in a way that truly demonstrates the breadth of your writing skills.

The type of responses I've always gotten from this approach are small advertising agencies who want free consultation about a writing problem. Few freelance writers I know of get the kinds of assignments they want through ads.

The best way to select clients is to determine the type of company you'd like to work for. We already touched on this in the chapter, "Evaluating Your Market Potential." The public library is a good source of background information. So are the lobbies of big businesses and ad agencies, chambers of commerce, and Fortune Magazine's annual list of the 1000 largest industrial companies.

Also find out what advertising and public relation agencies are in your area. Medium to small size firms are your best bets for freelance work. Very small agencies and very large ones tend to handle their own writing. Find out who the printing companies are that service companies in your area. They have a good knowledge of who has the budget for printed materials. If money is being spent on printing, there is a budget for production, and a writer is needed.

Put together a list of companies, including phone numbers, addresses and some information about their products and what they do. These are all potential clients. Now you have to find the people in them who can give you assignments.

Referrals and Networking

The best client you can get comes through a referral. That referral can then turn into many—not just one—new leads for work. Here's an example of how this can work:

A graphic artist I work with occasionally gave me a call. A family restaurant was doing well and wanted to update its image and redo its menu to appeal to a wider audience. A writer was needed to rewrite the menu.

I reported to an introductory meeting. The menu rewrite was easy, and through the project I established a rapport with the client and family. All went well, and as this project was coming to a close, the restaurant owner made the decision to expand into catering.

Naturally, the catering business required its own menu and a small advertising program. I wrote the new catering menu and two ads to help get this end of the business rolling.

The restaurant family liked what I did and had me write three additional advertisements for local newspapers. Of course, the referring graphic artist did his part on each assignment and was happy to get the continuous flow of work.

The family restaurant continued to do well. We were sitting talking about them opening a new drive-through business when it came up that a catchy name was needed. The freelance business writer side of my brain clicked in and ten minutes later I had devised a snappy name. They liked it.

Since the meeting was ended, I wrote the name in my calendar to remind me what it was and when I had made the suggestion. Then I wrote the name on a Post-It ™ Note and stuck it on his desk where he wouldn't miss it.

At our next meeting, the client told me everyone thought the name was great and asked how much it would cost for me to release the right to it.

I came up with a figure and on my next invoice included a fee for creation of the name. In the invoice, I released all rights to the name for his use. This way he had documentation that the name was his, and if trademark questions arose, he could use this to prove to another company the date that he started using the name.

The restaurant was not a big account. It was consistent though, and a pleasure to work for. They put very little pressure on me, which let me do my best writing.

It wasn't long before the owner gave me another surprise. He asked me if I knew he did a stand-up comedy routine. I had no idea. He thought I had a good sense of humor and liked the way I worked it into the materials for the restaurant. Then he asked me if I'd help him write a new half-hour comedy routine. Remember, all this began with a simple referral from a graphic designer that appeared to be only a quick menu.

I agreed to try to organize his comedy routine, working on a project basis. I couldn't guarantee that it would be funny and certainly could not be responsible for his getting laughs once on stage.

To get things started, I sat down with the man and talked through a range of subjects. It turned out that his family was a natural spring board for his humor. This is often the case with new comedians. We went over the material several times and he finally performed it for me, while I made suggestions about improving the presentation.

The stand-up comic/restaurant owner took his comedy to L.A. and the big comedy clubs there. He has continued to be a success, and the last time I saw him was on national TV, performing some of the material I had written.

You may not feel that your writing interests are quite this broad. You may not feel comfortable following up on things heading off in so many directions. However, it's good to know that referrals can open doors to exciting and diverse opportunities.

Ask for referrals to new clients and find imaginative ways to grow from one project to another.

Continue to keep in contact with existing clients even when you don't have a current assignment. Call them up and inquire how everything is going. See how campaigns you were involved with are working.

Beware the Discouragers

There was one person I contacted by telephone about writing film scripts. He was supposed to be the best in the filmmaking business in my area. I was able to get an appointment with him and arranged to come down to his office. After a short introduction, he spent five minutes telling me that my chances of making it as a freelance writer were slim to none.

He substantiated this by telling me, at length, that it was difficult, if not impossible, to make a living doing what I wanted to do. This was not a friendly warning. I got a heavy-duty, industrial-strength, very discouraging lecture about how bad my prospects looked.

At first I was a little shocked. I'd come in to see the head guru of industrial filmmaking and had gotten a lecture about what a dork I was trying to make it in an impossible business.

Figuring that I wouldn't want to work with someone as difficult and preachy as this, I stood up to him. I told him, "I'm going to make it. I may be the only survivor in the entire freelance business writing market in this city, but I will be the one who survived out of all the writers here."

I went on to tell him that I didn't need his approval to write and that there were plenty of other clients around and it was just fine if he wanted to try to discourage me.

He looked taken aback. He paused for a minute, then said that he always gave this little talk to people because he wanted to help thin out the ranks of those wanting to work in the film business. He thought the field was too cluttered with people who spent a year throwing pots, then a year in a dance troop, and then a year in some other art—such as industrial filmmaking. "They are riding through life on a pink cloud," he said.

He told me how impressed he was that I could stand up for myself and promised to use me. In the months that passed, I followed up. Twice I took him out to lunch, though both times he talked about himself, never asking what I was doing, what new skills I had developed, or how I could serve his writing needs.

Finally, I called him a last time to check in, and he said, "I have been using good writers who turn in their work on time and charge reasonable amounts for what they do. I just don't need anyone else." I thanked him and swore never to talk to the jerk again.

There is no reason for a potential client to lead a writer on. If they don't have any work, ask them to tell you that. Don't put up with people trying to discourage you or waste your time, and don't be afraid to stick up for yourself.

Your Clients Are Your Secret

Sometimes it seems that everyone in the world wants to be a freelance writer. And the impression is projected that many would-be freelancers are quite willing to do anything they can to get clients—even if they're your clients. Protecting your clients from others can be a subtle art, but you have every right to protect your income sources, subtle or not.

It's interesting to share work experiences with other writers. Nothing can be so cathartic as mulling over with friends a grizzly project that you just finished. There is also nothing worse than having mentioned the name of the company and person you work for and then have them visited by the writer-friend you told the details to. Or by some friend-of-a-friend who hears that there's work to be had from your client.

To some degree there is a code of honor among freelancers. If you hear that someone you know has called a client of yours, by chance, looking for work, you are well within your rights to tell the freelancer they are already your client. Politely call the freelancer and say, "Hello, there seems to be some misunderstanding. You are aware that (name) at (company) is my client. I'd like it to remain that way, so I'll let you know if they have any extra assignments I can't handle. In the meantime, I'd appreciate your staying away from the people I'm already working for."

Don't mince words when someone is moving in on your territory, whether it's accidental or not.

All the same, be polite and professional.

Other things can happen to put your relationship with clients on shaky ground. A common occurrence is another freelancer coming in and trying to undercut your price. Budget-sensitive clients may consider cost over everything else. The bad thing is that a client can always get the work done cheaper. The same is true for plumbers and for every other thing they buy. If cost is more important than issues of quality, on-time performance, and reliability, you don't need that client. Let them go with someone cheaper.

If the cost factor comes up, don't get into a bidding war with a competitor. You'll lower your price until there's no way it will be worth doing the writing.

It's wise, most of the time, just to keep your mouth shut about who you're working for. When talking with people about your assignments, describe the companies you work for by industry types. That's enough detail for a lunch-time conversation.

When You Move

Sometime during your career, maybe many times, you will move. As disruptive as this can be, it's a wonderful

105

opportunity to let your clients, past and future, know you're alive and kicking.

As far in advance of your move as possible, have your stationery and business cards redesigned with the new information. Create a moving announcement to go with them. This provides people with your new address and phone number. It also reminds old clients that you may still be available for freelance writing work and encourages them to refer someone in your new area to you.

In the announcement with your new address and phone, include a list of the types of writing services you provide. This will warm up old relationships, refresh current clients' memories, and turn up some new leads that could pan out into something good.

Chapter 8

Fees—How Much to Charge

How Much Will You Make?

Count on it taking a year to get established in freelance writing. If you aren't willing or able to take that amount of time to give it a try, you'll probably fail.

Some people have been lucky. Things have fallen into place because they've been hired back on a freelance basis by the company they used to work for. Others have stumbled into a major client or discovered a specialty field that makes them hard to replace. In general, though, figure on one full year to find the right clients, to get into the swing of things and to have a reasonable income.

After you've gone through this establishing period, you can make $20,000 to over $100,000 a year. This range of income is common for a full-time, freelance, corporate communications writer. Of course, you can always earn less. And that may be the way you'll want to do it. An article here and a brochure there to make extra income while concentrating on your personal writing.

On the high end, this income level range may seem very large to you. Especially if you're used to putting your heart and soul into an article for a small magazine and being paid a couple of hundred dollars for your efforts.

Let me emphasize again. Business is where the cash flow is. Particularly in companies who manufacture products rather than just sell services. Product manufacturers are used to spending large amounts of money for all aspects of research and development.

While great opportunities are available, realize that you can't jump in and get instant success. You will develop your own way of working and accessing the cash flow that is available to freelance writers in your area. How much you make is entirely up to you.

You Deserve to Be Paid Well

Everything may be going great at a client meeting, and it's only when the conversation comes around to how much you're going to be paid that things get touchy.

It is important to keep one thing in mind when quoting a fee for a business writing project. This is that you deserve to be paid for your work. You can draw your fee guidelines from a variety of sources.

To establish your fee structure, call some local advertising agencies and ask them what they charge for services. Ad agencies will have a feel for the market, charging the full amount the market will bear. People in ad agencies love to talk about their work and all that goes into it. Many of them enjoy talking about it more than they actually like doing it.

Call a couple agencies and ask for the creative department. Or ask for the head of their writing staff. A creative director, graphic designer, or staff writer will likely spend all the time you want telling you about the state of the ad business, their accounts, what freelance writers they use, and may give you some leads to boot. And you'll get a feel for what you can charge for your writing.

Ad agencies will usually bill more for their creative services than any freelancer dares. But they will also know what an independent freelance writer can charge. Once you're sure your rates are within range, don't hesitate to charge what you're worth. The worst thing you can do is charge too little. This gives clients the wrong impression about what they should be paying. After you bill the client too little, you feel that you've cheated yourself. It's interesting, too, that in business, if you don't charge "enough," they don't think you're any good. In many cases, the more you charge the more they think you must be worth.

So somebody says, "Oh, I can't believe how much you charge. You're the highest priced writer I've ever hired."

A good response to the high price label is, "You can always find someone who's cheaper, but I doubt you're going to find the same value or get as good a product." If you get tired of that line and are sure they won't take it wrong, you can always say, "I know what I'm worth, and I know what I can charge in this market."

With some experience you'll be able to tell what a client can spend on a project. If you feel that what they have to offer is too little, or if the demands they'll put on you aren't going to be worth the price they're willing to pay, don't accept the assignment.

It's much better not to accept the assignment than to get into the middle of it and want out. A client can rationalize your being too busy to take on an assignment, but will blame all the problems in the world on you—and never have you work for them again—if you bomb out in the middle of something.

Again and again, you'll hear a client say they can't afford more than a small amount for a freelance writer. This may be because they think it is an unnecessary expense or that writing isn't that hard. After all, some think anybody can write.

If you reach the point where they are claiming to have a small budget and you seem to be stopped in negotiations, take a moment to look at your client and think about how they spend money. That person likely thinks nothing of booking a last minute cross-country flight for a business trip. These are the most expensive air tickets you can buy.

He'd put himself up in a fancy hotel, charge meals to an expense account, and live it up while on a business trip. If he has any personal expenses, he may very well let the company pick those up quietly through a petty cash fund. Yet try and ask that same person for an extra $100 on an assignment, and you get nowhere. He is likely to act like you're trying to embezzle the money from him.

Another way to stick it out for more money is to compute what you think your client's salary is and what it would be if they were paid the way they want to pay you. Calculate the hourly rate offered and multiply it out over a 40-hour week. It'll turn out to be very little money. They would refuse to work for that piddling amount. Still they may want you to write for that little money.

Listen closely to clients to hear what they really mean when establishing your fee. What does it mean when they say, "You're just too expensive." It can be a signal that you aren't appreciated. The client doesn't realize the skills you have to have to do your work.

Look for warning signs when selecting clients or working on projects. There are clues you can pick up that will tell you if your time is being wasted.

On the same token, watch out for clients who take pot shots at you. It is rare to have a client be overly complimentary. Some may even jokingly run down your work. And don't be surprised if your achievements are forgotten in the rush to get a project completed.

If you never know where you stand with clients, they are probably not making an effort to make you feel safe and secure. They may not have decided themselves how they fit into the structure of their own company. They project that insecurity on you. Worse, some might secretly like to be freelance writers, but fear they couldn't cut it.

Charge Backs: Additions To Your Base Fee

While most of what you charge for is your time, there are other expenses you should be reimbursed for, and this should be understood in advance.

• Messenger services save you time and money. They can speed a new draft of important copy across town while you're working on something else. When a client wants something fast, send it by this type of courier—at the client's expense.

• Your client may want a copy of your writing on a word-processing disk so it can be sent to the typesetters who will plug it into their system and set type from it. That company will use your keystrokes to set their type electronically. This saves your client money and makes the accuracy of the typesetting flawless. Make it clear there is a surcharge for this.

• Unusual travel should be billed. You drive 40 miles to a plant site. There you interview experts on the subject of your new audio-visual program script. You have lunch when you're there and dinner on the 40-mile drive back. Your mileage and meals should be reimbursed.

There must be a clear understanding with the client that the charge for your time and any out-of-pocket expenses are two different things. Your time involves writing, research, and related activities. Expenses are directly related costs you have a cash outlay for.

If you purchase something that's used for one client's project and used again for other client work too, you'd best prorate its cost. For example, I was asked if I could bring in a diskette from my word processor so a typesetter could use it to set type.

This made sense, and I brought it in. My system used one type of diskette while the graphic design firm I was working with had a different brand computer that used different disks. They were incompatible.

The way around this was to telecommunicate the data file. The client asked if I could modem the information to them. This way, I'd electronically send the data from my word processing computer, over telephone lines, to their mini-computer.

I didn't have a modem but said I'd look into it.

The alternative was to have my diskette reformatted so that it could be read by the graphic art firm's computer.

The charge for formatting a disk was $450.

That was going to be just the beginning of the charges. After they set it up, there would be an additional charge for each disk that was converted from my computer to theirs.

Here's how being alert to situations and thinking of creative alternatives can help your freelance writing business grow. I purchased a modem and had it installed. One week was necessary to get the proper information about modems and determine what software communications package would be needed to make it work.

The software was new, so it took several days of experimenting to get it in sync with the modem, since it needed special modification to operate properly. Then the graphic arts people and I worked at sending the 54-page document over the phone lines for two days before we transferred the data intact.

All this trouble for what?

When I invoiced the client on this project, I charged them for half the cost of the modem and software. They paid half of my $435 cost, which I rounded to $220. This saved them the difference between my $220 charge and the typesetter's charge for setting up the disk formatting, which was $450 alone.

The modem gave me new capabilities. After it was installed, I could send information to the same graphic arts firm and directly to typesetters.

Soon I began working with other graphic artists and art directors who had computers. I'd modem the copy to their computers. They'd code it with information for the typesetter and send it on to them.

Another benefit was the growing number of resources available through modems. Data banks continue to grow in number and in the scope of their resources. I could tie into everything from news sources and library files to theater listings and want ads.

On every project since, where the modem was used, I've charged back a percentage of the original modem cost to the client using the system. Even after the initial investment was paid back, I continue to make the charge on my invoices. This way I can build a fund to keep my equipment current.

Another thing the charge back does is make the client fully aware of what you had to do to get the project finished.

Keep careful track of your out-of-pocket expenses on a project. Also watch for opportunities to serve the client better while constantly improving your service. And be sure to have them pay what they should back to you for your expenses.

You'll have to decide how you will handle some potential charge backs. The only time I bother keeping track of gas mileage and recharging the client for it is during a long trip over 50 miles. Otherwise, I just build the cost of operating my transportation into the writing fee.

Some writers count miles and charge for them. Every time they drive ten blocks, they have to keep a record of it. The amount of reimbursement can't justify the hassle involved. I frankly don't feel it's worth the effort and would rather build in those costs.

Getting Involved in a Corporation

You become a part of the organization when you take on a business writing assignment. Take advantage of this as much as you can. Use their long distance lines to do your out-of-town research. The company's photocopying machines are free, so use them. Collect the things you need copied and bring them in. I've never heard a single complaint about overuse of a company's photocopy machine, these are such common office tools.

Look for other perks too. You deserve them, so use them. The company may have a store where their products are discounted. They may have other things you can take advantage of, such as reduced prices on tickets to concerts and sports events, travel, or a newsletter used to sell things.

There is no reason why these extras shouldn't be available to you. So long as you don't break the rules, what's the problem? Anything they can provide to make your writing go more smoothly, and your life easier, you should pursue.

When They're "Not Going to Pay You"

Educating your clients is critical. The more they learn about the way you work and what you need to do your job, the better your work will be. And the more they know about the information you need, the more satisfied they will be with the projects they assign you, because they will be able to more easily recognize what they want.

Beware of clients who don't understand what you're selling them. Some believe that all you're vending are sheets of paper with words on them. They want to pay you for the price of the paper, which they don't see as being worth very much.

Your client has to know that you are selling your time.

So, what do you do when a client decides that your invoice isn't going to be paid? This occasionally happens with clients who don't work with freelancers much, or if a personality conflict has arisen.

They might tell you, "We're not going to pay for it because we didn't use it." This has been heard by freelance writers since the occupation was invented, right at the dawn of literacy.

Respond simply to this simpleton, "I charge for my time, I don't have any control over your use of the material I wrote for you."

Watch for other reasons why a client is reluctant to pay your bills or wishes to mark it down. Be calm and cool. Don't antagonize or get mad. Simply explain how you feel

115

about the situation, then tell them again that you are a professional freelance business writer. You provide your clients with more than words on a piece of paper. You sell your time and expertise, just like anyone else in any other business.

My experience has been that, faced with the reality of the amount of time you've put into a project and a careful explanation of the work you do, they will acquiesce.

Invoice and Be Damned

Sometimes you have to get out of a project. When it happens, it is most often because a client is being uncooperative.

I had a client who wanted to change the scope of his business to include a new line of products and related services. We were on cordial terms. I'd never gotten along better with an individual on a writing assignment. I'd write a draft, we'd go over it at a meeting, then changes would be made—replacing a word here or there. I'd go back to the word processor, grind out the changes, and messenger over a clean draft.

With the new project, things were different. I'd hear that the client was out on his boat—for sunny inspiration rewriting the copy, putting in Shakespearean quotes and horsing it up.

We'd have another meeting and it was as though the entire project had begun anew. The relationship was always friendly and nice. We never argued or criticized each other, though I did make it clear that the major changes were because the client had a change of mind.

Changing minds is common with people who don't do much writing—or reading. They have trouble seeing things committed to paper. Writing something makes them feel that they are stuck with what's on the first draft. They don't realize that writing is open to revision. You can't magically climb into their heads to extract and straighten out what they're thinking about in such a discombobulated fashion, but you can try.

In this project, I rewrote the assigned brochure copy for a sixth time. That was enough. When I handed in that draft, I told the client that I'd had enough and that an invoice would follow.

This worked out. He knew that revisions were because of the lack of decision-making on his part. The invoice was paid in short order.

There may come a time in a project when you've put in enough time. It's clear that no matter how much more you put into it, a *final* draft of the copy will never be approved.

There is a dark side to this. The client may decide that you are the problem. You are the reason the project is not being completed. Now is the time to be up front and stand your ground. Sit down and talk through the steps you've taken to complete the project. Make it clear that you have done your part to see the writing process through and you don't feel you can go any farther with it.

If things seem stuck, you can ask for a partial payment on the project. This means you intend to go on trying to give them what they want—but need them to begin investing in you. Or take the bolder step of asking to bill out completely. This means they are free to ask another writer in. This may mean you have lost the client. It might be that you don't care. Stop and consider: if it's this much trouble getting copy approved, are they worth the time you are spending on them?

Whichever tack you take, think through the ramifications of it. Determine how the client will react. And consider how your future income might be affected.

Discounting Your Charges

This happened regularly with one client, a small advertising agency. They were too small to have a substantial staff of writers or designers, so they farmed the work out. They had taken on a client much too big for them and had broken the work up among several people in their organization.

I was brought on to do some writing, but the agency would not allow me direct contact with the client. This indicated a problem. They were pretending that people at their agency were doing the work themselves. They were always calling at the last minute with small assignments that they'd put off. This didn't seem to be a big problem, in fact it looked like they could provide a good steady income. I had cultivated the account by taking individuals out to lunch, calling, and dropping by for the small talk that ad agency people thrive on.

And I kept getting assignments.

"Oh, you're such a good first draft organizer," they'd coo. Then they'd take my draft which had smoothed out the problems in their concept and had worked the major thoughts through the important information points. After a couple of quick rewrites, they'd get all the credit and most of the cash.

Finally, a few days after one of these rush jobs, I got a call and the ad agency person said, "The client wasn't satisfied with the approach and doesn't want to pay the $250 you quoted."

I said I had a policy of not reducing my invoices, but in this case reduced the bill $100 because of assurances of a huge amount of future work. The promise of a lucrative tomorrow is an appealing come-on and is often used to get a freelance writer to reduce a bill.

The next week the agency lost the account. I wasn't surprised, given their disorganization. They let a dozen people go—and the person who had been promising all that additional work was on the phone to me, asking for freelance writing leads so she could make ends meet while looking for a new job.

The rule is—never mark down a bill after you've quoted a price. Don't let someone balance their budget at the expense of the person most easily manipulated—the freelance writer.

Chapter 9

Managing Your Writing Business

The Business of Business Writing

Freelance writing for corporations is a business. All writing is—if you intend to be paid for it. This doesn't make your business writing less important than your other types of writing. It doesn't mean you've sold out. You'll find that the more businesslike your approach to your work, the better the assignments you'll get—and the higher the quality of all your writng.

Actor Bruce Dern expressed a similar thought in an interview. Success that he is, Dern said he wished he had paid more attention to the business of acting. He thought that being the best actor he could be would gradually bring him the parts he wanted.

It didn't work that way. It took concentrating on the business aspect of acting—in his case the proper agent, packaging of his image, and other factors—to really bring him the parts he wanted.

Likewise, a serious approach to the business of writing for businesses will bring you more interesting assignments. It also frees you up to do your work—and gives you less to worry about.

People and Systems that Help

When you start freelancing you have to develop your own system for handling your finances. Whatever system you develop, make financial management a primary concern.

Staying financially afloat can be tough for a writer. The money issue always rears its ugly head. Keeping your financial ship on course when the cash starts flowing can be an even bigger problem.

If you're used to struggling along with your writing, earning little from it, it may come as quite a surprise that a consistent cash income can be established with good business clients. Going from an on-staff job to freelance means that suddenly you're dependent on one company here and another there. One pays in three days and you never have to worry about them. Another may have to be reminded in 60 days just to get the payment wheels turning.

There are many ways to handle it. Here's what works for me.

The very best thing to do is find a good, solid accountant who has experience working with self-employed people. The accountant's experience is invaluable. A good one is a cross between a mathematical wizard, wise Tibetan Lama, and drill sergeant.

I was lucky enough to get an accountant who works with graphic designers, writers, photographers, and many other people in the marketing and advertising industry. His partner is a woman, newer to the trade, but with quickly maturing skills. Together, they are fantastic at taking any simple question I may have and giving helpful examples of how similar situations were handled. Their approach is very comforting, not to mention very knowledgeable and complete.

Find a good accountant by asking other successful self-employed people who they use. An accountant's experience with people in the arts, business communications, and related businesses is invaluable to you. Interview accountants as you would interview any employee who was going to work for you. Find out what kinds of clients they have. Ask if their tax returns are audited and how often. Discover what the results of those audits are.

You want good, safe advice. While you want to pay what is fair in taxes, you want to take full advantage of the existing laws.

The first year I freelanced, I assumed that my own bookkeeping procedures would be simple. After all, I couldn't make all that much money, and what could be complicated about going back through my checkbook to pick out business expenses from the personal purchases.

Ha!

What a surprise. I didn't bother to copy invoices or log in when they were paid. I kept that information on slips of odd-size note paper with a paper clip on the top. At the end of the year, I spent days figuring out what I made and rechecking it to make sure it was accurate.

My cash expenses were on receipts, but some of the receipts weren't dated and didn't have the name of the business on them. They were no good unless I could prove where they'd come from. I threw many of them away.

That was like throwing dollar bills out on the street.

To get by that year, I ended up making huge lists of every category of expense. Pages and pages of yellow tablet paper went into the effort. I sat for an hour with my poor accountant explaining what I was trying to get at with all the scribbling.

Fortunately, it came out all right.

The next year, I started with the yellow tablet paper. I copied invoices before they went out, so I had an exact record of them. I listed who they were to, the project name, date issued, and amount on a sheet of paper. The far right column checked them in with the date when they were paid.

This worked for the income part, but the expenses were nothing more than a huge box of receipts, slips, stubs, airline tickets, and every other sort of piece of paper and form.

At the end of the year, I spent three solid days sorting through all the pieces. Then I clipped them together by category and placed them in a large manila envelopes.

The contents of each envelope had to be listed on yellow tablet sheets and explained to the accountant—who was very understanding and accepting of all this.

The next year gave way to an accordion file. This is a series of tabbed slots in an expandable paper file. It can hold an entire year's worth of receipts by category. Discovering the accordion file was like finding the lost treasure of the Sierra Madre. It was the total resource for saving all those sheets of paper and keeping them in order.

But as much as this helped give the paperwork some rhyme and reason, I still didn't have the information in any easily reviewable form. So days were eaten up making lists of all the receipts, and presenting them again on yellow tablet sheets with long explanations.

When visiting my fabled accountants again, I finally had the presence of mind to ask if there wasn't some better way to keep track of all this information.

"Oh yes, yes, yes," they enthusiastically answered, as if they'd been waiting for this question from me for years.

The accountant showed me a "write-once" accounting system. These come in different styles and are made by different manufacturers. Mine is a McBee folding book-keeper system sold only through their representatives. You can find a McBee rep in the phone book. Inside the metal lined folder are checks arranged so that what you write on them copies to the correct slots on the accounting paper underneath.

Using a "write-once" system, you never miss a check entry. To the right of the spaces where the check information is entered is a series of columns. Each is labeled with a category of expense. By noting the account of the check in the correct column, all that needs to be done is to add the columns up. Hourly clerical help or the accountant can do that quickly.

This type of system is so simple and helps organize the nonaccountant so easily I wish I'd asked for help earlier.

I sit down with my bookkeeping every couple of weeks— if I remember—and make sure I've updated all the information. At the end of the year, I take out all the sheets and hand them over to the accountant.

For cash expenses, I have a separate book. And for invoices, I have another. I note how the cash was spent in the separate column.

Breaking Even

What I find really evens out income is not the number of assignments I get; it's their size.

Small assignments are time-consuming and don't pay that well. I see them as builders to larger assignments from the same client. You can seldom bill for the full amount of the time you spend on small projects. Even by establishing a minimum fee.

I figure this theory is similar to the merchant who can bargain on very expensive items a lot, because there's enough room in the price to give a little. The merchant stands firm on the lower prices because the margins just aren't there. In some stores they sell a lot of stuff cheap. In other places, they sell a few items at high margins.

I decided to try setting a minimum for all assignments. A minimum writing charge of $500 seemed fair to me. If I had to make two trips to the client's office—assuming the first draft of the material was acceptable to them—and added the time I spent writing and rewriting, $500 would be the minimum break even point.

The theory didn't work. All it did do was give me an easy out from taking a couple of assignments that came along that were too small. Having the minimum also let me beg out of working for a client I felt wouldn't be worth the trouble.

In reality, if a client asks for a small assignment to be written, you can really only charge what is fair. This may end up being whatever they have in the budget. Usually writing something short, say the length of a one-page press release, might as well be done by the client. The reason a freelance writer is being called in is because they are disorganized, or because they can't face the task of doing the writing themselves. Sometimes you are performing a gigantic service to take this small hassle off their shoulders. But what's a drag for them will likely be a drag for you, too, if there's no money to be made in it.

When you accept a small assignment, make sure they know you expect to hear from them when a bigger project comes along. As my freelancing progressed, I upped my stated minimum to $1,000. I figure that they had better be willing to invest that much in the writing before I'll make an investment of my time in them. But quite honestly, I'm flexible about that if I need to be.

Financial Accounts and Contacts

Separate personal and business finances by keeping different accounts for each.

And save money.

These steps, and building a good relationship with a banker, are the ways around the constant questioning of your financial status.

Shop around for the financial institution that can serve your special needs. Banks, credit unions, and savings and loans are often competitive in all of the services they provide. Establishing a business relationship with one person at the bank who knows you well can make all the difference between your getting the service you need when you walk in and being sidetracked into a mass of red tape every time you want to cash a check or take out a loan.

Applying for a mortgage is complicated for anyone. Because you're self-employed, you have to be evaluated as an individual. This is something mortgage lenders are not used to. They have spent years categorizing people and just can't stop themselves. Freelancers don't fit into neat little categories and can't have their income checked with a phone call to a company personnel department—the way normal people can.

Get to know a banker.

What has worked for me is keeping my personal checking and savings accounts at my neighborhood bank. There I got to know the loan officer who has helped me considerably. I regularly keep him informed about my writing business. Every year I give him copies of my tax returns. With this information, he is able to give me loans and handle my banking needs without a hitch.

At times I've needed 30-day notes. Other times I've needed loans for a word processor, automobile, and all the usual things people need.

Getting to know a banker is a big plus.

However, I keep my business checking account with a brokerage firm. They give me the best interest on cash there. This includes checking privileges, and I can also buy and sell stocks within the account. Every month I get a nicely organized statement and I can call the broker to chat and see how I'm doing.

Banking regulations are changing constantly, allowing every sort of business to open financial service operations, from department stores to stock brokers. Shop around for the financial institution that suits you best. Study the accounts they offer to see which fits your needs. Get a feel for the personality of the place and the individual you'll be working with.

Your income is going to fluctuate. That's the nature of our work. You want to continue to build your cash reserves throughout your writing career. Begin these savings right away and stick with it, always adding to them.

Some experts say three-months worth of cash is a good amount to have in reserve for emergencies. I'd say a freelance writer is going to feel much more secure with at least a six-month cushion. My goal has been to have a liquid cash reserve to support me for an entire year if I stopped working.

Incorporation

The most common reasons to incorporate your freelance writing business include protection from liability and additional options for managing your money.

What you write for companies will be read and approved by your clients many times before they use it. So the chances of your being liable for something they approve and publish are slim. The issue of liability, or need for liability insurance, is probably not too great a concern.

The issue of liability would most likely come from a client finding that you released inside information you learned about their company during the course of your project research. This could happen because you may be privy to proprietary information about products or processes. Knowledge of this information could theoretically be worth millions. Clients extend a lot of trust when they let you in on company secrets. You will usually be asked to sign a confidentiality agreement to be certain you understand that you cannot divulge what you learn.

Even if they sued you for revealing information, they would never be able to recover anywhere near what you have cost them. So incorporation for protection from liability is probably not an issue.

Image may be a more valid reason to incorporate. In some businesses, a corporate name presents greater credibility. To give your operation the appearance of being a solid, reputable firm, incorporate and give it an appropriate name.

"Graphic Identity Group Incorporated" has a trusty ring to it, while "Judy and Dick's Art and Writing Service" lets on that it's just the two of you working out of your front room.

I don't think you need a business name if you're going to freelance for business. You want to get your own name in front of your clients as often as you can. Make looking up your name in the Rolodex file as easy as possible. You could lose business to someone else if you can't be found easily. With a business name, your client might forget what you're calling yourself and not be able to find your phone number. In my case, I went from "George Sorenson Freelance Writer" to "Sorenson Company Incorporated". I'm still filed under "S" and easy to remember.

If you incorporate, the premier reason for it should be financial. Your accountant can review your income, expenditures, and other factors, and determine if incorporation is going to save you money.

I incorporated after three full years of freelancing. Even then, my accountant said it was a toss-up. It's a matter of examining the numbers to find out if its more profitable for you to write through a corporation. Incorporation for me means I get my invoices paid to the company name, and the company income is reported under a Federal Tax I.D. number instead of my social security number. My social security number is used on my personal taxes.

Being incorporated hasn't increased my business. It has given me more flexibility in handling income and expenses. It's helped me keep my bookkeeping better organized. Better organization is probably its greatest benefit.

Chapter **10**

Doing the Work

How Much Do You Have to Know?

One of the many good things about writing for business is that you usually don't have to know anything about the assignment topic when you begin. The company that gives you the assignment is full of information and ready to put you into touch with people who will give you everything you need.

Often business writing demands nothing more than some basic organizational skills and common sense. You will quickly find out that many people in business lack these simple qualities. This is especially true when it comes to organizing a client's thoughts, determining what they want, and getting it down on paper. This is why they call you in and why your assistance is so needed.

Frequently, freelance writers working for a company outlast the people working at the company full time. This means that the writer has greater knowledge about the company's products than some of the newer people there. It's not unusual for a business to have you informally training new employees because you're more intimately familiar with their products and services than anyone else.

Your work there, researching and following through to complete a writing assignment, has given you knowledge of their organization too. You are a valuable asset to the company.

Don't believe you have to know the subject in advance to write about it. But make sure they remember how valuable you are to them once you know their products and their company.

The Concept Meeting

Unfortunately little is done in business that doesn't involve a meeting. When receiving an assignment or bringing in copy for review, you're likely to be obligated to attend a meeting. There is no single secret to making these a success. Group meetings are seldom necessary and generally accomplish very little, while still taking the greatest possible amount of time.

One thing can help. That is leading the meeting yourself. Don't confuse this with running the meeting. When you're given a writing assignment, you've been brought in to organize things for people. They need leadership and direction. Because you're a writer, you know what's involved in gathering essential information and making it work in a piece of business communication. The meeting is the place to show this.

Here's my approach. Begin by asking questions that lead your clients to reveal the information you need. Oddly enough this is not always forthcoming. Ask what audience you are to try to reach. How are you asking the reader of this material to respond? What is the most important thing you want the person reading this to come away with? What sort of first impression are you after? What is the format, tone and approach that should be taken?

It can be absolutely startling how much trouble people have getting this basic information out and organized. It can be difficult for them to identify what is important and what isn't. This is especially true if the company, or the individuals, haven't had much experience creating written materials.

Sometimes you want to say, "Come on, I know you're hiding something. What do you really want in this brochure? You can tell me. Go ahead. What should we tell your reader in this piece?"

Another thing that can be useful in getting the most out of meetings is careful scheduling. Holding a meeting an hour before lunch can help you considerably. An 11 AM meeting is perfect. It limits the meeting's length because the unheard lunch bell sounds in corporations promptly at noon. Limiting the length is excellent since nothing much is accomplished in a meeting lasting more than ten minutes under any circumstances.

It also allows your client to ask you along to lunch, maybe in the employees' cafeteria, where you can meet other people from that corporation and expand your business. These lunch rooms are usually well maintained, with reasonably priced food. Here you can chat about things other than work and get to know the client.

One gigantic privately held corporation I work for has a dickens of a time getting committee approval on anything. They are so cautious about their company image they issue annual reports without a balance sheet. They don't have to make their bookkeeping public, so they don't. It is just an image piece, carefully written, rewritten, and edited into the ground.

I've done slide-show scripts for these people that have gone into five and six drafts. This happened because they would only release information that needed to be in the show when they saw it was obviously missing from my script.

"How come you didn't include the big grain elevator in Louisiana?" they'd ask.

"You never told me you had a big grain elevator in Louisiana," I would respond.

Sometimes a client can be so familiar with information, they are unable to explain it to you. This is particularly true of old-timers who have been with a product since its inception.

There is something melancholy about someone who has lived with one product during his entire career. The product was new and important when he was hitting his career prime. Now that product has been surpassed by new technology. And the person is thinking about retirement. This individual knows more about the product than anyone on earth, but there is precious little that's new he can think of to tell you about it. This is one of the toughest assignments you can get.

What do you do if you recognize this type of client and product and expect it to be difficult to work with them? The easiest thing is not to accept the assignment. But then, a freelance business writer enjoys a challenge, likes to work hard to please a client, and is ready to get in there and be creative. So go ahead and try it. Make the assignment work for you by finding a new approach only an outsider could see.

Tons of Material Needing a Focus

You will usually be given too much background material. You can walk out of a meeting where you've been given a writing assignment with a pile of literature so tall it looks like you're cramming for a law school exam.

Some of it might be useful to your assignment. Much of it will be repetitive and boring. The most important information you'll get from the client is in what they say at the meeting. Not what they give you to read.

The questions you ask them and the answers they give will be the central information in your writing assignment.

The reason you're given so much information is mostly the client's inability to determine what's important. Learn how to evaluate what is important in what the client tells you.

Learn about the company and what direction it's headed. Often an entire corporation—especially the big ones will have a specific ad focus. Sometimes these will go for years on end.

We saw this with the "quality" emphasis programs. Everyone had to stress quality in everything they did.

The quality message broke down into several elements: "satisfying the customer's needs" and "doing the job right the first time"—things like that. For three years, corporations across the country couldn't get enough of the quality message. Then it throttled back and the push was on for an "entrepreneurial spirit."

You'll find that the clients look for references to their current corporate emphasis in your writing. Find out what issues are being pushed by your client. It might be the need for innovation. Safety might be the current hot issue. Whatever it is, be aware of it and work it into the copy.

Listen to your clients for quotes. Use their wording to describe important points in the finished copy. Whether they recognize their own words or not, the copy will sound familiar to them and make them feel comfortable.

Getting the Work Started

There is always pressure to get an assignment finished quickly when writing for a business. Much of the anxiety can come from the client giving you too short a time frame to complete the project. Or perhaps because you've taken on too many projects. Assignments pile up and soon you're swamped.

You'll find that no matter how overloaded with work you get, you can lighten your work load and speed your writing along by following a few suggestions:

• Realize that your client has probably given you too much information. This is common. Start working from your notes and only refer to the mass of printed material when necessary.

• If you don't have enough information to complete the project ask for more. Call your client and explain that you need more input to complete the project. Present an expanded outline that includes the information you already have to help the client identify what's missing.

• An outline is the key to meeting deadlines. This is because the raw data you have to write from is generally in no particular order. It's likely that it's drawn together from a dozen sources: different people, reports, meetings, brochures, and off the top of your client's head.

• A good solid outline of the assigned writing project can get you through nearly any meeting. If a first draft is due and it is just impossible to get it together, talking through a detailed outline of the information can usually satisfy the client that progress is being made.

Working Fast

The quickest way to handle business writing assignments, I've found, is to prepare an outline using a yellow or off-white writing tablet. These are easy on the eyes.

Use standard 8-1/2" x 11" size. Don't use 14" legal-size tablets. They're too long and won't fit on regular photocopy machine settings. The sheets stick out of files, won't fit into interoffice envelopes or in and out baskets.

Pile the wealth of material your client has provided next to your tablet. Go through it quickly, using one word or a short phrase to create the outline. Place the information on the tablet page in the position you expect it to fall in the document you're writing. Material that will serve as an introduction gets placed at the top of the page. Interesting body copy that will move the middle section along is arranged where you feel it should be presented. Jot down a code for the source of the information.

Facts that sum up the information are naturally placed at the end, along with concluding thoughts from your client.

Your writer's instinct will tell you where to place the information in your outline. An outline like this will allow the assignment to organize itself.

One piece of paper might not be large enough to get down an entire outline, so lay out two or three or more blank pages and follow the outlining process across the several sheets.

Once this rough outline is complete, put the original information aside and type the outline. Use several pages again, typing each outline entry with about an inch or two of blank space beneath it. Then take this typed rough outline and elaborate on the information. This can be done with a pencil—sitting in a building lobby when waiting for a meeting or on a plane when there's no space to do anything else.

I've found that an outline that successfully hits the main points of the material, and that has been reviewed by the writer and client to fill out the information, is a good base for creating a solid first draft. The only faster way to work is simply to sit down and type a first draft. That's possible with material you're familiar with, but difficult (and not recommended) with newer clients and unfamiliar information.

Every business writer will develop his or her own method of digesting information and getting work done quickly. Working with an outline is one method to do the job fast.

Making Demands

Demand that a client be faithful. If they're going to use other freelance writers, you should know this. If they give you one assignment, ask for another. If you haven't heard from them in a while, call and ask why not.

When you hear that they're using another writer, complain about it. Find out why they didn't call you. It could be that they just forgot or that some other person in the department made the call, not knowing about your experience and abilities.

Keep your profile high and ask for what you want.

Writing and Rewrites

Two natural laws of freelance business writing:

1. Cranking out a first draft is the hardest part of the writing process.

2. The whole secret to successful writing is rewriting.

The thing that most people have trouble with is getting their thoughts organized and down on paper. You'll find that until a client sees a first draft of your work, it's difficult for them to focus on what they want.

You sometimes hear, "You really missed the point." Or, "No, this isn't at all what we wanted." Chances are your client didn't know what they wanted in the first place. People are always ready to tell you what they don't like. Presenting a first draft allows you to get the reactions you need to complete the assignment.

Nebulous instructions are common. Because business managers were busy in school learning how to manage, they didn't learn the proper ways to criticize the written or spoken word. Imagine a college English student's class reaction to a professor's suggestion to make something they wrote "crisper" or to "brighten it up." This criticism does nothing to provide specific suggestions for change. Still, this is the kind of reaction you are likely to get from a corporate client.

It is difficult for most clients to criticize your work with any specific articulation. For example, clients will tell you that they want a "high-quality piece." They might also give other useless instruction, such as "make it professional." Sometimes a client will order rewrites for no particular reason at all. The only criticism is that you've written something that "doesn't feel right."

It's interesting what some car dealerships do when a customer brings in a vehicle that "doesn't feel right." They park it overnight in their repair lot and do nothing to it. The next day, the owner returns and takes it for a spin and thinks it runs fine. You can't do that with your writing, but often time helps.

Conversely, it is a treat to have a client who is capable of expressing thoughts about something you have written in an intelligent manner. If you find those kinds of clients, hang on to them. You'll produce your best work and will get far greater satisfaction from the relationship.

Don't make the mistake one would-be freelance business writer did. Across the top of his stationery he had printed in big red letters: "Don't Change A Word." And he backed that up by resisting and arguing about every little change anyone wanted to make in his copy.

I once met this writer at a company where we were both doing business. The client later told me that the writer lived up to the headline on his stationery. He turned out to be difficult to work with and didn't have the flexibility to handle rewrites cooperatively.

He never worked for that company again.

I did.

When They Edit You

The editing you get in business communications is unlike anything you've seen before. There is little consistency between clients. Some are able to pinpoint exact words that need to be changed. Others want something to be different but are unable to tell you in what way.

Businesses don't edit in the conventional sense. You seldom get back a draft with changes marked on it. There are usually notes stuck on, no changes at all, or just a couple of corrections.

At times I've gotten back a draft of my writing with changes indicated. I've taken it back to my office and made the changes, smoothed out some other points in the copy and handed it back. The next time I'm in, a new person has reviewed it, and the pages are covered with marks that look like an interstate highway system map. Whether the writing is acceptable depends totally on who's doing the reading. Sometimes what one person will criticize on your draft will have more to do with the politics of the office than what you wrote.

One company I worked for over a long period had no particular system for approving copy. Once something was written, photocopies were distributed to ten or twelve individuals. Each one of these people had to have input. The result was chaos. No one met the deadline for returning revisions. Copies would get lost. The whole process was just plain stupid.

The problem was their internal organization. It was impossible for them to make decisions. No one person could grant authority for approval of the writing. There were no guidelines for what was to be said in the materials.

I'd get back twelve copies of my first draft with changes from twelve different people. I'd put all the changes possible into a second draft. This meant that some people didn't have their indicated changes included because theirs contradicted the changes of others. Because some of these "editors" saw that their changes weren't made, they blamed me for missing them. Each one needed to be talked to, very carefully. I had to take care to massage their egos while working to create an agreeable final draft.

This Neanderthal system of copy approval was frustrating. My client—the marketing manager to whom I reported—tried to avoid sending out copies of the first draft.

He would take my first draft and have it type set. This would be included in a formal layout. This completed keyline was circulated and changes noted on it.

The slew of people who had to review the material was much less likely to change typeset copy than a photocopy of typewritten material out of my word processor. The typeset copy had a certain formality and finality. It made them stop and think about how important a pondered change really was.

Companies don't really edit. They change and rewrite. There is no standard system for this. You need to create a system for your client if there isn't one.

Working as an Editor Yourself

There is editing work in business writing, too, although most of this is done by the people responsible for the creation of the work. Much of what a company produces in-house can be edited down in length. Many things produced there should be cut in half or made even briefer than that. Many written documents aren't professionally edited because people in a company don't understand what an editor does— or how one can help.

Corporations believe that a project they've completed is uneditable because it was written by their experts in that field. This is clearly not the case. Often experts know so much about a subject they don't know what's important. What they write goes on and on, never getting to the point the reader cares about.

Go after editing assignments with the same zeal, and using the same methods, as you would writing assignments. This type of business writing work will be much less obvious and more difficult to find. One of the reasons is that your clients won't be thinking about hiring out editing jobs. And the work they do that is of a length that would require an outside editor doesn't come along very frequently.

The major editing assignments I've gotten have come from nowhere in particular. Once, a company was producing a training guide by tacking together previously produced materials from a variety of sources. The project coordinator literally cut apart sections of competitive manuals and taped them together.

Because there were so many writing styles joined together in the materials, there was no flow to the writing or consistency to the terms used in it.

The project became available because I was hanging around the company's marketing department for a meeting on another subject. A beleaguered worker from the training department stopped by to chat. We discussed writing issues. She asked for some advice about the project.

"Maybe you need an editor to bring all this material together for you," I suggested.

"What would that do?" was the uninformed response.

I went on to explain that I could unify the material into a single cohesive piece. This 300-page training manual could be read as a complete book and no one would have to know that it was pieced together from so many sources.

"Gee, OK. You mean you could do that?"

It worked wonderfully. I went through the stack of material and marked it up. A secretary typed the changes and gave me the draft back.

When I was done with the third draft, the length was reduced to 220 pages. They were very happy to pay less for typesetting and printing, and they saved considerably—even with my fee.

Should you charge less for editing than for writing?

I charge the same for editing as I do for writing. Other freelancers charge less for editing, but I don't see a big difference between the two types of work.

It depends on how much of the "editing" becomes rewriting. When estimating an editing bill, read through the document thoroughly. It is very easy to underestimate the time required to straighten out someone else's writing.

Deadlines

Deadlines for freelance assignments are unreasonably short. There are few exceptions to this rule and many reasons for the constant state of tension this creates. Most of it is the result of inadequate planning and endless procrastination on the part of the people giving you the assignment.

You can cause deadlines to be tight, too. A freelance writer's workload can cause a project to get behind schedule. All writers are guilty of waiting until just before an assignment's due before working on it.

One reason a writer puts assignments off until just before their deadline is that it gives the subconscious the maximum amount of time to churn over the information. I find that working on a project is a process that begins as soon as the client first mentions the subject matter to me. The subconscious begins to digest the information as your client explains what the assignment is. The tendency is to wait because the longer your subconscious mind sifts through the material, the better it's understood and the easier it is to handle. At least that's what you tell yourself.

There are other reasons why a business writer waits until the last minute to go to work, adding substantial deadline pressure. For one thing, the project may not be all that interesting, so other more exciting things are tackled first.

It's like eating the things on your dinner plate you like first and saving the overcooked lima beans for last—hoping they'll magically disappear before you get to them.

Many times a particular project may seem so complicated that other smaller projects ought to be done first to make way for it, or it seems too overwhelming to attack.

I've found, instead, that doing the big or unpleasant project first gets it out of the way and allows me to do the smaller projects with even greater speed.

Any way these assignments are approached, having the ability to change a schedule around is critical. Even then you receive assignments that keep you from going to parties or doing other things you want to do. Dinner invitations have to be turned down because work has to be done. It also means you can get into a rut, working all the time and just barely keeping up with deadlines. When you're so busy you only have time to scurry from one deadline to the next, tightly making each one, it's called "putting out fires."

Consider the different ways you can set deadlines and meet them.

When dealing with clients, you'll often need to set the pace for a project. It may be your responsibility to impose the deadline on the project—and on your client.

Here's a typical scenario. You find yourself in a meeting where everyone knows they need a writing project finished. They will all agree that it is important, and they're glad they brought a freelance writer in to handle it.

All the information will be presented to you. The client will shake your hand and smile and send you off to do battle with your typewriter. When they receive your first draft, the group will sit on it. They'll hand it around to everyone in the office and generally let their momentum fizzle out.

You want to turn in a well-written project, and you want to get paid. This isn't going to happen until the final draft is approved. But the client isn't moving on the project and it looks like you're never going to get to the rewrite.

Here's where you can impose a deadline. Say, "I need a deadline so I can set aside time to finish the rewrite. When should we meet again?" Explain that you bill at the end of the month and if the project can't be wrapped up and all the final approvals gotten, you'd like to bill anyway.

Or if the project's stalled, send a partial bill. Billing half makes the client invest something in the project, and consequently they have more reason to want it completed soon.

Deadlines and billings are critical to you. Deadlines, because they let you plan your time; billings, because they provide your sustenance.

The two are inseparable.

Placing a deadline on a project helps get the client organized. It gives them a realistic expectation of what they can expect from you. And it helps you manage the project along with other demands on your time, allowing you to do your best writing.

Saying "No" to Monday Deadlines

"When can you have this finished? Today's Friday, how about first thing Monday?" The worst thing you can do to yourself, unless it is completely unavoidable, is to promise anything on a Monday.

Remember what's involved when you promise to have writing finished on a specific day. If it's due Monday, you're going to spend your weekend working on it. You're better off having it due on a Thursday or Friday. This gives you week days to work on the project. And it saves your weekends.

Getting time off on a weekend is hard enough. But when you're committed to a Monday deadline, this is what happens:

Saturday, you will look at the material and plan it out in your head. Sunday, you're in church (or ought to be, perhaps) or watching a football game until the middle of the afternoon. And then, Sunday night, until the wee hours of the morning, you will be typing away. If questions come up, no one is available at the client's to answer them.

Monday morning, the energetic freelance writer drags in to the client meeting with the copy still steaming, it's so fresh from the typewriter. A good percentage of the time, people will be missing from this critical meeting you worked so hard to make. And that copy that seemed so urgent Friday isn't so important Monday morning.

Save weekends to recharge your batteries and catch up on life. You deserve the time off to pursue other interests.

Hurry Up and Wait

Many times you'll get an assignment because someone else has procrastinated. They thought they'd do the writing part of the project, too, and at the last minute decided they couldn't handle it themselves.

"Oh, let's call in that freelance writer what's-his-name. He's real fast and can write this and get it back to us overnight, I'm sure. No problem."

No problem for them, but a big problem for you. When the phone rings, you're supposed to drop everything, trot down to their office for a quick meeting, then hurry home to crank out their copy overnight.

146

A client might ask you to be at their office in 20 minutes. To get you to accept this quick and often low-paying work, they may promise tons of future assignments and then deliver nothing. You might never be able to get them on the phone again after the current rush assignment's over.

Whichever way assignments are handled, let your client know what you have to go through to get them done.

If it's a rush job and inconveniences you, make that clear to the client. Explain to them that there will be a rush charge added to your usual fee if their time demands are too extreme. Don't take it for granted that a client recognizes this or expects to compensate you for it. Quote them the rush price before you accept the rush assignment. In the heat of trying to get a project done, it's easy for a client to demand a lot. The "hurry, hurry, money's no object" attitude is pervasive when a big project is underway. It's another thing to get them to pay for the trouble they've created for you once the project is done and the pressure is off them.

Most freelance business writers will agree that the people hardest to get payment from, and the ones who will put up the biggest fuss about a big bill, are the clients who have made the biggest demands at the last minute.

Handing in What You've Written

I always like to read the material I hand in to the client aloud. Usually I can point things out they don't recognize. And often, if there is a meeting with several people involved, it's best to read the copy to the group.

When I read the copy like this, I can put some of my own inflections into the work. Everyone in the meeting will hear the same things in the material in the same way. When this happens, people are more likely to indicate what changes they want in the copy in a useful way for you because you can ask them questions. In the meeting setting, they will have to justify what they don't like in front of the people they work with if they request a change.

Sometimes someone will say they have to think about what they've heard. They might also say, "It's not right, but I just don't know what it is that I don't like."

In meetings, it's also common for people to get on the boss's bandwagon. One influential person saying, "I don't like it," can lead a group of "yes men" (and "yes women," of course) to agree that they don't like it either.

The presentation at the meeting is the perfect place to pin people down and ask, "What, exactly, would you say in place of what I've written?"

You see it's easy for a corporate bureaucrat to say something isn't right. It's simple for them to criticize and put the brakes on something you've written. It is something else to stick their necks out and say what they feel should be said in its place.

When beginning my freelancing career, I used to hand in what I'd written almost with an apology. I had built up in my head the arbitrary standards of high school and college English professors who over-criticized everything I wrote. Most people's experience in having writing criticized is in a literature class where even literary giants are ripped to shreds.

When I started out, I didn't have it in my mind that I was a professional writer, doing a job. The feeling of being a student handing in an assignment hung on long after leaving school, and the first couple of times I handed in professional assignments, I pointed out all the deficiencies. It was my way of apologizing for my lack of self-confidence.

I'd say, "Here's a first draft. There were a lot of things in it I didn't understand. There's an awkward transition here, and that information there may be inaccurate."

Sure enough, whenever I'd tell the client that I was missing certain types of information or knew I'd misinterpreted parts of the material, I would hear exactly that criticism back in a few days when we would meet. It was as if the client had not read the material—which I think was sometimes the case and just relied on the evaluation I'd provided along with it.

Criticizing your own work aloud to a client creates a self-fulfilling prophesy. What you say is wrong, they'll tell you is wrong.

Don't fall into this trap. When handing in a first draft, flatter your client and yourself at the same time. To do this, don't tell them what trouble you had organizing and developing the material. Make the feeling positive.

Realize that what you have written is probably better than anything anyone else on their staff could turn out in the same period of time. It certainly has more insight into the product or service because you are on the outside of the company looking in. Add to this the attitude that you took the pile of information they gave you at the last minute, or the inadequate amount of data they scraped together, and forged a solid working draft from it.

Now, feel proud of what you've done. Ignore the fact that you barely got it finished in time. Forget that you only skimmed it quickly once for typos, and get rid of any other doubts.

Go in there and give them the copy you wrote and say, "This is the great first draft that I promised you. It craftily catches all the points you wanted. It is absolutely perfect. This isn't to say we won't want to change a few things—I'm ready to rewrite, you know that. But please realize that this is a great start."

I have done this a hundred times and every time the rewrite was easy. The times I'd gone in and been straightforward about what I think I'd change and what was weak, it only added to my client's anxiety and made the rewriting and approval process take longer.

Create confidence in yourself. Tell them you really worked at this writing and that you're presenting them with something that will do the job for them. This is good Karma, and the good positive feeling that comes from it will make a big difference in how you and your freelance writing work are perceived.

With clients I've worked with a long time I even go farther. I say, "This is the best writing I have done in my entire career."

They laugh. But it gives them confidence that helps create a trust in the good job their writer has done.

Working with Other Vendors

Writing can be a lonely profession on the whole, although business writing is more collaborative than many other types. Usually you work with other people throughout the process. Sometimes this means managing your clients' time and helping them make the best use of their skills, as well as your own.

As a writer you have the advantage of being able to organize the project. You are often the first person assigned to work on it. You often have the opportunity to dictate—if that is not too strong a word—the direction the project will take. You have the maximum amount of creative influence.

In this working relationship, you are, of course, a vendor to your client. In turn, you may work with other vendors. These might include a designer, photographer, printer, and other professionals. The client may have people who have worked for their company before. These are familiar, reliable vendors who are known and trusted. Or you might be asked for suggestions about which vendors to use for design, photography, and other related services.

Finding a good graphic artist is the most frequent request from a client. This graphic artist or art director helps the client decide what visual appearance a printed piece will have.

If you're producing a brochure, it could be a single, double, or triple fold. You will have to work closely with the graphic artist to see that your headlines and the length of your copy fit into the space available. When creating an audio-visual production (such as a video tape or slide show) many creative visual decisions must be made, too, titles and the use of drawings, photos or other visuals.

The freelance art director sometimes has not learned as much about the product as the writer has learned in the course of writing about it. He usually relies on a brief explanation from you or a quick read-through of your final draft copy as his primary exposure to the product or material. This isn't to say an art director isn't interested in the topic or won't make an effort to learn about it. Often copy is received at the end of the production cycle, without the time necessary to fully digest it.

Some of the best contacts you can make in the freelance world are with graphic artists. They are often approached by clients with an idea for a project. Sometimes, they get an entire package of work that can include brochures, direct mail, and advertisements.

While the artist develops the look of the creative product, an artist still needs a writer, and you may be called in to write the copy.

And there's something else you can try with graphic artists. Rather than calling them up and showing them your portfolio so that they can keep you in mind for an assignment—do the opposite. Make an appointment with a graphic arts firm to interview them and see their portfolio. Tell them that your clients occasionally ask you for graphic artists and you need to get to know some new ones. This way you are a potential help to their business. Suddenly you are a professional peer and not just another freelance writer trying to make a living.

If they get a call for a writer, who will they recommend? You: the freelancer who has promised to try send some work in their direction.

Something else I've found: because I work with words, I'm better at making presentations than most graphic artists. They seem to try to let their work speak for them. Some graphic artists ask me to come along to do the talking at meetings. Still a client is more apt to spend time on the visual layout of a piece than on the writing.

Here is a very real problem you face in your freelancing. Your client will more readily understand what the graphic designer is doing than what you are writing and how it can be changed to express their information satisfactorily.

Keeping this in mind, search out good, solid graphic artists and art directors to work with.

Another vendor group you'll want to know is photographers. They won't have the same ability to send you clients because they're usually involved in the creative process after the design and writing has been done.

However, you will be asked at times for suggestions about photographers to do work for your client.

Sometimes you can suggest a specific vendor that you know is right for the project. Other times, it's better to suggest two or three, arrange for the client to see their portfolios, and let the client decide whom to use.

Like graphic artists, some photographers are better at some things than others. Some shoot only architecture, some products. Others shoot food, which is a specialty. Food photographers have to know how to make food look delicious, and they use a bounty of tricks. Other photographers shoot only on location. Still others have a large studio and have to support that overhead with a constant schedule of studio shooting. Some work well with people and do fashion work or specialize in character shots.

Get to know several photographers. Use them to help develop the network of vendors you can recommend to your clients. These vendor-friends can also pass along your name when a freelance writer is needed.

Chapter **11**

Sample Assignments and Fees

I'll Show You Mine If . . .

These are some of the types of assignments a business writer can expect. Briefly, this is how these were handled and the amount I charged for them:

Two-Fold Brochure

The workhorse of the corporate communications business is the 8-1/2" x 11" sheet of paper that has two folds in it. The resulting brochure neatly fits into a standard #10 office envelope. You see this size brochure by the dozen on bank counters, in muffler shops, and everywhere else.

Through a referral, I was asked by a small company to write a two-fold brochure. The company, a manufacturer of industrial machinery, had invented a new machine and wanted to promote it.

I called in a designer I work with and we went down to the company to discuss the project. We were taken on a tour of their workshop and asked what we could do.

After having written scores of this type of brochure, I had settled on a standard charge of $800. The amount seemed to be a comfortable figure for my clients, and it was for me so long as the project didn't take too much time.

However, I added another $200 to the assignment by writing a press release as a part of the project. Total Fee: $1,000 Total Time: 6 hours.

Periodical Article

A leading investment journal contacted the public relations department of a medium-size computer company. The editor wanted an article under the byline of the CEO of the company on how he saw the automated office taking shape.

Computers were really hot just then and there were articles everywhere speculating what the future would hold.

Naturally the chief executive officer wasn't going to roll up his sleeves and draft a thoughtful article. The request for the piece was funnelled to one of the PR people who knew my work through the company's marketing department. I had made a point of getting to know the public relations staff, just in case an opportunity like this came up.

The call came in at 2 p.m.. They wanted the article back by 10 a.m. the next morning for their review. I was down at their office at 4:30 that afternoon to pick up the information and stayed up until one in the morning drafting the piece. I then hit the sack and was up at six to rewrite it.

At ten o'clock on the dot I handed in the article. There wasn't any time for me to be involved in further rewrites, so it was time to invoice them for the project.

The periodical this article was headed for was influential. The amount of pressure on me to crank out a good, workable draft of the article was huge. On a straight $75 per hour rate—which I quoted at the time—I calculate I would have charged about $750 for ten hours. As it was, I was ready to bill them $1,200 because of the rush of doing it, having to set everything else aside and work all night.

Before sending out the invoice I called the manager who assigned me the project. I mentioned the $1,200 figure with some hesitation, asking her opinion. She said it seemed a little high and I showed my cooperative attitude by backing off to $1,000. Not bad for one night's writing work.

The article got stuck in the approval process in their PR department and missed the deadline. It was never run. I was paid anyway. Total Fee: $1,000. Total Time: 10 or so hours.

Motivation/Training/Speeches

The call came from a casual acquaintance in a large company. We had met in the office of another marketing communications person by chance months before. I had taken the opportunity at that meeting to give her my business card and say, "When you need a freelance writer, what're you going to do? Call the number on the card."

In her office was a middle manager who oversaw the activities of 150 sales representatives. These reps were responsible for selling three basic products, each related but with different applications.

He needed a speech to give at a sales meeting. This event would be held in a desert resort in the middle of winter. The participants would be coming to the meeting thinking about their golf games, not about their sales figures.

The speech was to last 12 to 15 minutes, refresh the reps on their products, and motivate them to get out and sell more.

The middle manager was willing to take some chances with the presentation and suggested it have a western theme. This seemed a bit corny, but he was willing to try it, and he probably needed all the attention-getting devices he could get to keep the audience interested.

I met with the man twice to get background information on the products. Then I drafted an outline and reviewed it with him. The outline passed inspection, so I incorporated the changes he suggested and began the first draft.

The drafting process didn't go too smoothly. The manager was traveling extensively, so I was seldom able to talk with him. I would leave a draft in his office and he would take it on his next trip to review it. At one point he left a corrected draft on an airplane and lost it. This set us back, with me rushing him a new copy off my word processor.

Weeks went by and we were getting close to the due date. Still I wasn't able to meet with him because he was gone all the time. I spoke with the woman who got me the assignment. She had talked to the manager and he didn't feel the writing was going well. She asked him, "Is there any problem other than you're traveling all the time and aren't able to meet with the writer?"

He said no. So my problem became raising his comfort level about the writing by increasing the level of communications between us.

This problem was solved by the manager sitting in his hotel room and dictating changes in the speech into a micro-cassette recorder. He sent me the cassette by overnight courier. I listened to it and made the changes.

Half-way through, I called in an illustrator who did cartoon-type drawings. He was able to pick up on the western theme successfully, and his drawings were transferred to slides to support the speech.

By the due date, the speech was in good shape and I delivered it and the cartoon slides.

The speech went over very well. The speaker wore a cowboy hat and got into the character of the thing, making it a success.

This is a project I wish I had charged more for. My fee for writing was $1,550. The illustrator billed the client directly and so did the company that transferred the illustrations to slides. I probably could have charged an additional $500 if I'd taken the trouble to add up my hours and considered what I had to go through to get the work done. What I could also have done is to have billed by thirds, so I would have been paid as the project progressed. Not a bad idea with a new client.

Total fee: $1,550. Total Time: 35 hours.

Direct Mail Program

A large real estate development firm needed a direct mail program to do two things. The first was to find companies who needed new buildings constructed. The second was to find smaller companies wanting to lease space in existing buildings.

I came on the assignment through a referral. The direct mail project was much too small for a friend who runs a firm that manages large direct mail programs.

Because the client was new to direct mail, I charged $3,000 for the first month to analyze their needs and set up the program. My agreement with them after that was to write a one fulfillment package to be used with a mailing program of one new direct mail letter to be sent out every six weeks.

The program would last one year.

Each month, after that first start up payment, I received $1,000. As part of my assignment I pulled together information about mailing lists, small vendors who get direct mail processed and related things. I began not knowing anything about direct mail, but I learned a lot about it, and have since been able to handle several programs for other clients. Total time: Monthly project. Total Fee: $3,000 the first month and $1,000 per month for a year.

Audio-Visual Script

An independent video tape program producer got my name out of the *Gold Book*. The *Gold Book* is a publication for my metropolitan area that lists all the people in the communications industry, including printers, photography, public relations, broadcast stations, corporate public relations, ad agencies, recording studios, illustration, art direction, and, yes, copywriting.

Such a book is a good place to be listed if there's something similar in your area. The *Gold Book* does not charge for the listing, and it is revised annually. It's also a good reference source for you.

The AV producer and I chatted briefly on the phone, and a meeting was arranged to discuss a script. It turned out to be for a petroleum exploration company. The headquarters was in my city, although their oil wells were in Oklahoma.

I met with the producer and the client to get basic information about the company. Included in the information were an annual report, brochures, and an hour of questions and answers.

Three days later I met with them again to go over an outline. Taking their comments, I wrote a first draft of the show. Here I was careful to write something that the producer could make into a video presentation and stay within budget. In this case, there was enough budget to travel to the oil fields, rent a helicopter, and do location shooting. The producer had the second draft in hand when he made the trip to shoot the footage.

Three weeks after we began the project, the necessary video tape was shot and I had refined the script further. I presented the final draft. It was approved and I invoiced the producer for the project.

Another three weeks later, the program was completed and the client was happy with the results of the 12-minute program. Time spent: Around 30 hours over three weeks. Fee: $1,200.

Chapter **12**

Stuff to Watch Out For

Working on Speculation

It's called working "on spec." The scenario is simple. A potential client calls you up. They have a project in mind and want you to come in and talk about it. At the meeting you get revved up about the prospect of this major assignment. It could be a catalog, article, direct mail program, or brochure, anything.

Everything seems to be going well. Then the axe suddenly falls. They either want you to write samples of the piece, or they want the entire project written so they can take a look at it and then decide if they like your style. And they want this done without any obligation to pay you for your work if they don't use it.

There are variations on this theme. A client might have you write one chapter out of twenty for a new software training system. They expect the work for free and the decision to pay you for your time to be made at their whim.

Your chances of getting paid for spec work are seldom good. You will probably do your best writing because you know it's being carefully scrutinized. The amount of time you'll put in will be monstrous because you want the rest of the assignment and know that payment is based on your performance.

In reality, things don't work that way. If someone in business is going to pay for new tires on the company truck with nothing more than a guarantee from the manufacturer, why should you not be paid for your writing with your guarantee that you'll rewrite the project until it is acceptable?

If someone in business really wants something written and they're willing to go outside for it, they ought to be ready to pay what it costs.

I know a freelance writer who rewrote one article seven times before the public relations client told him he'd changed his mind about the subject of the project. Since there'd been no agreement about payment and no commitment to accept the story, no money changed hands. The writer had an article that had little chance of being marketed elsewhere. The writer was just starting out and wanted to get his foot in the door, so he accepted an assignment on spec, thinking that would do it.

Some clients will never be satisfied with your work. If Faulkner, Shakespeare and Hemingway collaborated on it, the client would still find fault with the results. Knowing this about themselves, they will ask several writers to write samples of a project. The project could involve several descriptions of merchandise in a direct mail catalog or a great deal more. Only one writer will eventually be paid for the work.

While the majority of your clients—and potential clients—will be honest and tell you what they're doing, some won't.

I was called in by a big direct marketing catalog company. After an amicable meeting with the person in charge, I was certain, based on our conversation, that I was the star writer who would be creating their ambitious new catalog. It meant writing mountains of merchandise descriptions. It also meant a new catalog coming out every three months—with me doing the writing.

All my new client wanted to see was sample descriptions of some catalog items. The timing was tight, and examples of my work were needed in 24 hours.

Watch out when people need writing finished in ridiculously tight time frames. Also beware when you can't get them down to specifics on their budget, the timing for the project, or the names of the other persons you will be working with.

I burned the midnight oil, came up with several catalog descriptions, and paid a messenger to deliver them to my client. Then I waited. I called to be sure they had been received.

They had. "Wait a week," I was told.

So in seven days, I called back and got a secretary. "Oh, we're considering the samples and will select a writer soon." The statement was like a bazooka blast.

"Wait a minute, I'm glad to work with you to develop the style of the project, but I understood I was to do the writing."

"You must have misunderstood. We've had several writers do samples for us and we're going to choose one," the secretary said.

"No, excuse me, but I'm sure I didn't misunderstand. There was no mention made of this at all. My agreement was to write the catalog. The style was to be based on the samples I was preparing. I don't enter writing contests, so I want to clear this up," I responded, making every effort to be as cordial and convincing as I could, with no display of anger.

I called the client back a couple more times. I always spoke to the secretary because the client would never come to the phone. My samples were never returned and I eventually discovered another writer was selected.

The decision you have to make in these situations is whether to press your case. There are two choices. Either invoice the company for your time and be willing to press them for payment. Or write a neat little letter spelling out the misunderstanding, and hope to get work from them sometime in the future.

Since I could see little chance of ever working for the company, and the potential client was disorganized and self-aggrandizing enough to make the easiest assignment difficult, I decided to send them an invoice.

The invoice amount was modest. There's no point of trying to overcharge for a project. There's no reason to compound the problem with an unfairly huge bill.

When the client received the invoice, he suddenly became available for phone calls. Funny how that works.

"I'm voiding your bill," he said, and went on to disagree on all of the main points in our meeting about the project. He maintained that he had told me other writers were being considered for the assignment and that my samples were being done "on spec." I said he didn't, and we became locked in a stand-off.

At the end of the month, I sent his company's Accounts Payable Department an updated invoice that included a 1.5% monthly finance charge. In a couple of days, I received another phone call. The client was even more belligerent, said he'd "voided" my second invoice, and hung up on me.

Now the freelance business writer has to make a decision. Knowing that you're working in a close-knit community, is it worth getting the word out that you're standing up to a client over such a little matter? Or do you really want the satisfaction of proving that you're right—and getting paid for the trouble?

In most cases it probably isn't worth going to too much trouble. This is what clients who want you to work on spec count on. When I realized that I wasn't going to be paid for my time, an immediate option was to get the name of this person's boss and talk to her. Chances are that the two aren't on great terms. Based on the way I was being treated, I figured other people coming in contact with this individual were having problems with him, too.

And by the time I was ready to make the decision whether to press for collection I probably would have been satisfied with an apology. All I wanted was an agreement that there had been a misunderstanding. The client needed only to express some sympathy about the situation and I'd have let it go. I'd even have proposed we work together in the future.

I also knew that if I challenged the client effectively, it could improve what was happening to freelance writers in my market. There would be more respect of our craft and less willingness to treat us as less than full-fledged business partners.

In this case, I decided to file in small claims court because the client was so confrontational and nasty to me.

I won.

It's best not to go to court unless you absolutely have to. Ask your attorney for an opinion if you have the slightest doubt, and realize you're probably in for a long battle.

Better yet: Make it clear from the start you don't work on spec. Speculation makes you share the risk with a client, without the ability to share the success. Don't compete with other writers for work. These situations become writing competitions, held by your potential client who probably isn't a very qualified judge.

Working For Nothing

Once people know you are a professional writer, they will ask you to donate your services to worthy causes. Rather I should say, causes they *feel* are worthy.

People who would never ask house painters to work free or rug cleaners to donate their services will expect you to give them your writing skills in the interest of their charity.

Similar to this is the person starting out in business who feels that their own bright potential to make a killing in a new enterprise outweighs your right to be paid for your work. These entrepreneurs will ask you to create their new marketing literature free, with the promise of payment when they are a success.

Before you commit to producing writing for free—stop and think it over. When the person pops the question and follows it up with all the sincere, heartfelt warmth that radiates from someone wanting something free from you, take at least two days to think about it.

There is nothing wrong with donating your services.

However—know what you're getting yourself into.

It is amazing how picky people can be about things they feel are truly important. In non-profit organizations, there are often politics between the members who vie for power and position. All this stress can come to a head with your writing project.

When I was starting out, I did some volunteer writing to help build my portfolio. After a couple of pieces, I cut the amount of work I'd do on this basis to very little. It just wasn't worth the strain.

Take the same tack with the entrepreneurs who want you to share the risk. When entrepreneurs start a business, they'd better have a handle on the financial resources necessary to get the enterprise off the ground. The expenses they have in starting up their business ought to include a budget for marketing resources.

If they haven't thought through the marketing of their business, they'd better go back and take another look at it.

I've seen it happen where a guy getting a business going asked for writing help with the promise to pay for the services once the cash started to flow in his business. A freelance writer took the assignment and put a lot of time and effort into getting the material out. Eventually, the business did get off the ground, but the writer was never paid for the work, and the owner went to another writer for follow-up work.

Hesitate thoughtfully before giving away your work. At the beginning of your career, when you're building your portfolio, consider writing a couple of pieces without charging. After that, give it a big long think before committing yourself to something that doesn't pay.

Here's a test to determine if you should write on spec or donate your services:

First: Ask yourself if the project is something that really interests you. Decide if it's something you'd do without pay or acknowledgement.

Second: Find out if anyone else on the project is getting paid for their work. If the designer, printer, photographer, and everyone else are donating their services, then you know you're on an even footing with them.

Don't be the professional who is the only part of the creative team asked to work without being paid your proper fee.

167

Cancelled Meetings

A favorite saying of Louis XVIII was, "Punctuality is the politeness of Kings."

Old King Louie was right. You must be on time for meetings. If you only do one thing right for a client, make sure it is getting to their meetings on time.

On the other hand, if a client consistently cancels meetings with you at the last minute, there is a problem. If you show up for a meeting and they aren't there, it indicates a big problem: the lack of respect for your time.

If you have a good stable writing client, someone you know fairly well and can usually count on, you may let them cancel meetings without much fuss. I even had one who was so busy he frequently missed meetings. I'd show up and a secretary would explain that he tried to reach me, but couldn't, to tell me it was called off.

This was an unusual situation. This client was so great and well-meaning, I knew he made every effort to be there. Other things simply kept coming up at the last minute.

If you find that a client is just changing appointment times at a whim, and it's affecting your ability to do a good job, take action. First explain to the client that you had to reschedule a couple of other meetings to fit this one in.

If it keeps happening, tell the client that you will have to charge for your scheduled time, whether the meeting takes place or not. Explain that cancellations so abrupt that they don't allow you to fill the time with other clients will be added to your bill. Make it a "cancelled meeting charge," just as the dentist does if you don't show up.

I had one case where I never actually met a client. It began with a call that came out of nowhere. A person in a large corporation wanted to meet immediately to discuss a project.

I suggested another writer be called since I was heading out of town for a week.

The person said I sounded like the the right writer for the job and insisted on a meeting the next day. I'd get all the information on the assignment at that time. In a week, once I'd returned to town, I would meet again at a prearranged time and review the requirements.

At the first meeting the client was out sick. An assistant who had just come on board and didn't know what was going on tried to explain the project to me. It seemed simple enough and took about one hour.

In a week, I returned with a proposal for the project, including an outline of the information. When security called from the reception desk to announce that I had arrived for the second meeting, the assistant answered. She said that the client was supposed to have called me to cancel the appointment. He'd changed his mind and had her do the writing. There wasn't any assignment any more, and I was just to "forget about it."

The next day, I called the client to discuss the situation. Two hours of meeting time had been eaten up, plus, travel time to the company's office and back. That added another three hours to the total, easily. I at least expected an "I'm sorry, I forgot to call. My mistake, can you ever forgive me for the inconvenience. I'm sure we'll work together again soon."

But, no. Instead he was very nasty about it. He couldn't care less that I had come all the way there for two bum meetings. It was of no concern that I had to shove other appointments around in my schedule to make it to his office.

Had I gotten a simple apology and some understanding, I'm sure I would have said thanks and expressed my desire to work on a project together in the future.

In these types of situations, there are several alternatives you can follow. One is to call the person's supervisor. A supervisor will likely listen to what you have to say, note it for future action, and might also authorize paying you for your time.

A more direct way is to stand behind your professionalism. Tell the person this isn't how you do business, and let it go.

In this particular situation, the client was very rude. In fact, he hung up on me. So I simply sent an invoice at my hourly rate for two hours of time.

This triggered two more nasty phone calls from him. I shrugged these off, standing by my guns on being paid and letting the individual threaten me childishly with all sorts of retaliation. The result was my finally getting paid by the corporation. If you have legitimate grounds for your billing, large companies will often pay.

As long as you are honest and straight forward in how you decide to handle these situations, you can't really lose.

Self-Proclaimed "Good Writers"

A lot of people work for your client companies who would rather be doing something else. Some of them would like to be full-time freelance writers. They have already proclaimed themselves writers because they did well in English classes, or worse, they have some sort of degree they use to support their notion that they are competent at writing.

Watch out. If you are at a meeting for a writing project and are told by people involved that they consider themselves "good writers," you should wonder why they are not writing the material themselves. Also wonder why they

ed up their concern for the client without stating any
icular approach to the material.

he real problem was that there wasn't any one person in
A.V. firm I was to report to. Everybody in the
anization was afraid to take responsibility for the
erial, and everyone was so loaded with work they were
d all the time. Nothing was getting accomplished. It
ed out that the big successful audio-visual firm was an
anizational nightmare, barely staying ahead of its
llines.

he big mistake I made with them was to write a rough
t of one of the scripts, label it "First Draft" and leave it
one of their staff to review. I wanted to get a reaction to
material as I understood it because all the people on the
ect were headed in so many directions that there was no
is.

complained to the president about the treatment I
ived, and they decided they'd give me "one more
nce" to get the first draft right.

t the time I was learning the ropes and figured this
ation was common. Let me tell you it is not at all
mon and I was very much taken advantage of because I
ted to please them. Doing this, I sacrificed what my own
incts were telling me.

attended another meeting and got even more information
a rewrite. Then I stayed up all night and wrote what I
ight was a fine first draft. I turned it in and got another
ne call.

No, I'm sorry. This just doesn't make it. That's it,
're done."

was taken off the project because they said they didn't
the second draft either.

have to tell you this, rather than simply find self-satisfaction
in knowing it about themselves, and letting their knowledge
and craftsmanship in writing flower quietly during the
rewriting process. Clearly they have some insecurities
brewing that can bubble up and burn you later.

Listen for individuals who declare something on the order
of, "I consider myself a good writer. I have a B.A. and a
Masters Degree in journalism. I've been trained in the
writing craft. I lived and breathed writing for six years in
college."

If you hear this, and these quotes are practically verbatim
from an experience of mine, try to get up and run.

An example of this was when I was called in by a major
bank to write articles for their in-house publication. It was
basically a small newsletter, distributed to employees every
week. The initial two minutes of the meeting with the editor
went well enough. Unfortunately it was a ten-minute
meeting.

At first there were the standard hellos, exchange of
business cards and formalities. Then, out of the blue, the
lady began talking about her little newsletter as if it were the
Sunday *New York Times*. She positioned herself as the
editor of this flagship of periodicals, the editorial thrust of
which took its readers on a voyage to the deepest
understanding of the human soul, not merely through the
portals of employee retirement updates, bowling league
scores, and corporate trivia.

Needless to say, she preceded to give me her credentials.
Her undergraduate and graduate degrees were in journalism.
Consequently, she reasoned, everyone like her who worked
on newsletters like hers were "professional journalists."

Just between you and me, she worked for a bank. Period!
Now it's a big bank, so big it needs this little newsletter to

give everyone a sense of community. She may consider herself a journalist, and there's nothing wrong with that. But based on past experience, and judging from the tone of her conversation, I begged off from the assignments she was offering. My excuse was that the time frame was too short and that scheduling problems wouldn't allow me to do the job right. I knew that neither she nor I would ever feel satisfied with what either one of us wrote, said, or did.

Freelance business writing success is based largely on the chemistry between you and your client. Always look for friendly people with a good perspective on things. They're out there, even though it may feel like it takes a lot of looking to find them.

We'll Give You One More Try

Odd circumstances abound in freelance business writing. You will have a wide variety of experiences. You'll be able to travel to strange places: from a fire-breathing, smoke-belching factory to the rarified atmosphere of an executive board room where everybody makes over a million bucks a year.

Clients will fly you around in corporate jets. You will get to stay in every sort of accommodation from the worst flea-bag motels to super-nice, first-rate establishments. It can be great, if you're willing to put up with the down times and all the bends and curves along the road.

Strange occurrences may happen at any time. Imagine yourself in this one.

A very large audio-visual production firm was known to be very tough for a freelancer to crack. The one man who was supposed to be the contact for freelance writers was highly impersonal. He'd act as if you had awakened him in

the middle of the night when calling him work to introduce yourself. He was ab conversations, and just basically rude. I firm's president, but the calls were never re

I had been working on a potential c corporation for some time. This person ha budgets and periodically hired the audio-v been trying to crack. At a lunch meeting client, we ran into the president of the A. introduced to him. I greeted him and went tried to get him on the phone five time months to show him my work.

Of course, in the presence of one of his a little, telling me to call that afternoon for a

I did and ended up showing my portfolic him for an hour. The next thing I knew, so to someone else, and this man who was p called me with three assignments. Being president of the A.V. firm got me started could become one of their favored writers.

Immediately everything went awful. T been so rude continued that way. I opportunity to write a first draft on a single did one outline of an assignment (using th got a call.

"I'm taking you off these assignments."

"What's the matter?" I couldn't beli hearing.

"It's the writing," he said. "It just isn't an

"But, I haven't even been able to do any

And I hadn't. The only thing I'd been them was their tired old formula outline f

Something smelled fishy about this. There was nothing I could do about the projects. The A.V. company was so poorly structured, there wasn't anyone to discuss it with to really get to the bottom of it. So I billed them for my time. In a few days, I received a check for less than half the amount with a note from their accountant. The note explained that I didn't deserve more.

I sent the check back with a note demanding the full amount, with a complete explanation of how I had been treated by the people in the A.V. company, their lack of cooperation and absence of organization. I gave them a deadline for paying the full amount.

The accountant delivered the check herself with an apology. She was the nicest and most well-meaning of the lot.

To see if I was misjudging my own work, I took a copy of the second draft they had so soundly rejected directly to the client. He read it and said it was fine, just exactly what he had been looking for. He didn't know what the problem was with the A.V. firm and promised to follow up to find out.

I never worked for the big A.V. firm again. Never wanted to. What did I learn from this? Better yet, what can you do to avoid the same mistakes in your writing career?

The main thing is to trust your reactions to people. If the place you want to work is difficult to penetrate, it's likely that there's a reason for this. Either the company has overworked people who truly don't have time to talk, or they are chronically disorganized.

Do you want to work for a company that is an organizational mess?

No.

The person I was supposed to contact for freelance writing assignments hung up on me, was rude, and was a pain from the beginning. Where I went wrong was seeing this as a challenge. I wanted to beat him and get an assignment just to prove to myself I could do it—and to prove to them I could handle it. I reasoned that they were a big company and had the budgets to give me a steady supply of work.

The president of the A.V. firm had been the same way. He hadn't answered several calls and only responded when pressed by a client introducing me.

What am I telling you? Believe what you see and what you feel. If someone is tough to get along with from the start, it probably won't improve. Usually, when the pressure is on during a production, nerves get frazzled and tempers are on edge. How cordial will people be if they start out by being jerks?

And if they give you "one more chance," don't take it. You want a client who will cooperate and work to get along making your job go more smoothly.

Competition from Moonlighters

It can be disheartening when the people you are trying to work for are competing with you.

A major corporation has a communications department with writers on staff. The lead writer in this area tried to go out on his own once, but after a year of trying and failing at freelancing, returned to an on-staff job. Still he likes to pick up outside freelance work. So when the occasion arises, he does an assignment here and there.

I'd gone in and talked with this individual several times, making sure my name was out where it would be remembered—since he was in a position to give out assignments. One small assignment came through him, and that was about all.

Meanwhile, a steady client of mine suddenly had a couple of good-size projects produced—and I wasn't hired as the writer.

"So who wrote these?" I asked the client about some brochures. I feel that it's better to come right out and ask about these things.

"Oh, it was Mr. So and So."

"Geez, he works for this megacorporation in a full-time job. He would have had to do this work during business hours," I said.

Well, to make a long story short, the man was freelancing on company time. I didn't feel this was fair to me, since I don't have a stable salary supporting me. And depending on his company's policy, he may or may not be allowed to take assignments outside.

What do you do in this situation?

The first thing that occurs to you is to call the moonlighter and mention that the company he did the freelance job for is your client and you'd appreciate letting the freelance work there go to the full-time freelancer who relies on it survive.

This would have resulted in direct tension between a potentially powerful ally and me.

I considered dropping a note to his boss, inquiring whether employees were actually allowed to freelance on company time. That would certainly have gotten a response. However, they would have known that I had sent it, even if I didn't sign it. This would have come back to me somehow, probably in a negative way.

The action I took proved the best. I called the man up and asked to drop by to show him some of my recent work. The stated purpose was to keep him up-to-date on what I was doing a legitimate purpose.

In the portfolio of materials were some pieces from the company we had both freelanced for. I breezed through the material, including samples from the company, letting him know they were my client.

At the end of the short session, I thanked him and asked for some names of people in his corporation I could contact for writing assignments. It was a Fortune 500 Company with no shortage of freelance opportunities.

He gave me three solid leads to follow up and access to a usually restricted mailing list of marketing communications people within the corporation. He did this graciously and we ended the meeting amicably.

There's no telling if he'll do any more freelance writing or if he'll intrude into my territory again. He did, however, compensate me for the loss he had caused. And it was handled coolly, with no one getting hurt.

Taking On A Partner

At some point in your freelancing, taking on a partner will look like a good idea. You may want a partner when you realize you are spending all of your time by yourself in your office. So many hours will be spent alone that you'll pray that someone drops by just to watch you throw away a used-up typewriter ribbon, in order to validate the work you're doing. You'll even want to save mountains of rough draft copy to show people so they can understand how hard a writer struggles.

The money you're taking in will be good and you're just sure if you had the extra time that a partner could give you, your income would double or triple.

There seem to be many benefits to a partnership. It would make vacations easy. You could leave for a couple weeks and your partner could cover for you. Assignments could be split. You could diversify more and more, to the point where you could be doing the heavy thinking and not even have to mess with the boring stuff. Other people could do that. Maybe you wouldn't even have to do any actual writing. You could just conceptualize.

That's the good side. Unfortunately, I've never seen a partnership work between freelance writers. Freelance writing is a highly personalized business. Putting two people together and getting them to work successfully in a freelance writing relationship is next to impossible.

An acquaintance of mine freelances, specializing in public relations. She began the business with a friend. This "partner" was slightly older than she and had a couple of kids. When they formed the partnership, they realized that the older partner's kids would take up some of her time, and that my friend would be doing more work.

An arrangement was made so that one would get 60%, the other 40% of the net income. They then agreed on 25 other particulars about the way their business would be run.

They were sure they had resolved all the variables in the relationship and proceeded to have stationery and business cards printed. Office space was rented, clients were secured and everything started rolling along. Then reality set in.

It's hard enough to divide up work 50-50, even harder some odd ratio either side of that. When one partner was swamped, the other had nothing to do. One would start something and hope the other could finish it. Important deadlines were missed a couple of times. Soon nothing was working and my friend decided to go out on her own—and her partner decided to spend more time with her kids.

It wasn't long before they weren't friends any more. In weeks, their lawyers were handling their break-up. The woman with the kids demanded to be bought out for cash. But the problem was determining what the business was worth. How do you put a price on your clients? It's practically impossible to assign them a value, much less figure out what they're worth when you split up afterwards.

Their partnership lasted less than six months. It took over a year to resolve the disputes.

Partnerships take all forms. A certain writer wanted to maximize results. He organized three other writers to do work for him and offered translation services as a side line. He said he wanted writing partners, but really wanted to have other people do his work. This venture lasted two whole years before collapsing. It couldn't provide the personalized service or cope with the financial rock and roll of freelancing.

It is amazing how complicated simple situations can get. I entered into an informal partnership once. It began innocently enough when I contacted a marketing executive at a large company.

The fellow seemed like a good contact. He didn't come up with any work immediately, but he had an interesting way of looking at things that was appealing after exposure to so many conservative business people who were all stuck in the same rut.

What eventually happened was that he began asking me for freelance writing leads so he could build a business and get out of working for the big corporation. Just about then I ran into a large direct mail campaign I didn't know how to handle. I made the connection for him and he got the assignment to do it.

He reciprocated with a major assignment from the company he was working for full time. And things were rolling.

Soon we felt like partners: looking for work to share, meeting socially, and increasing the time we spent together.

Fortunately, we never formalized the relationship because everything started to go wrong.

He began showing up late for client meetings. When we had to meet, he only wanted to get together after eight o'clock at night, and always at my house. He became argumentative. And the person I once thought to be deep thinking with expansive marketing knowledge turned into a guy who was a dreamer—someone who couldn't buckle down and do his work.

I stopped giving him any of the work I was finding. Our lives drifted apart and we lost touch. So much for partners.

Although it is difficult and lonely working by yourself, alone is the only way to write. Unless you want to start a public relations firm or an advertising agency, partners are usually more trouble then they're worth. Sure, work with someone on a project now and then. But establishing any kind of permanent partnership between freelance writers goes counter to the nature of the work.

Watch out.

The Lure of Expanding

You will quickly see how much opportunity there is for you in writing for business. The temptation to expand your writing business to include other activities will grow very strong at times.

At some point you're going to want to turn yourself into an advertising agency, adding people who can do many different tasks such as reception, art direction, sales, or other services. This could mean more money. For sure, it means more complications with payroll, work loads, client hunting, and lots of overhead.

Remember the freelance writer who decided he was such a success that he could orchestrate the activities of several other writers? He'd go find the clients, get the information, and take it back to the office. There, a hearty bunch of writers would sit and wait for him to drop the material on their desks. They'd churn out the copy and he'd trot back to the client with it.

I've never seen anything ruin a writing career so fast. The ghost writers couldn't go directly to the client for information. There was no consistency of style between the writers.

It didn't take long for his little organization to collapse under its own weight. Some of his writers stole clients. The writer went back to freelancing solo very quickly and ended up spending more time getting reestablished than he took starting out his career in the first place.

Getting Sidetracked

Avoid the temptation to diversify away from what you're good at unless you've thought the whole thing out and have seen someone else do the same thing before successfully.

Watch for meetings where everyone falls into alignment with their boss's ideas.

Writing is a very personalized service. Don't dilute it with other things that look like they'll improve your income.

Having seen a detailed four-color running trail map of Central Park during a trip to New York, I knew that Minneapolis needed something similar. There is an extensive trail system in this Minnesota city, with bike paths and running trails covering tens of miles. No high quality map existed which showed the paths that thousands use everyday and others would like to know more about.

All that I needed in order to make a lot of money was a well-designed, colorful map of the main routes. Because it would show mileage accurately, it could be sold to everyone from beginning runners to experts. Everyone would buy it. All households in the city would stick it up on their refrigerators.

To produce one, I worked with a printer who had in-house design capabilities. The printer spent hours putting the map together accurately. I borrowed a bicycle that was specially set up for clocking race distances from a running equipment store. In a pouring rain, I rode all the routes on the map to make certain the mileages were exact.

Before we went into production, I did some marketing research on the project. I did this research the same way I make contacts for myself when looking for freelance business-writing clients, and I presold the map in small quantities.

The buyers were a local book wholesaler, a popular chain of running shoe stores, and a major book store chain. The professed "director-of-map-buying" at the bookstore chain was enthusiastic about the project. He made some suggestions to make it even better and promised an initial purchase of a quarter of the press run.

It looked promising. The map would be a sure winner. The money would soon be rolling in, stabilizing my freelance writing income.

I pushed the design group to get the art work done, and I had the map on the press as fast as I could get them to do it.

As soon as they were finished, I called all the people who promised to order and made sure that they followed through on their purchases. The fellow at the bookstore chain told me he'd placed his order. So I sat back and waited for the checks.

A month later, the maps sat in my garage. The big bookstore order never came through. When I called the "director-of-map-buying" who was my big supporter, I discovered he'd moved out of state. He had suddenly pulled up stakes and was gone, leaving paper work strewn across his desk. My order was not in that mess. Five thousand copies of my jogging map waited in boxes for distribution.

What happened? I was feeling so sure of myself as a business writer that I overstepped the limits of my own expertise. Because I worked with graphic artists and printers, I thought I knew their work better than they did. I thought I knew distribution, sales, the works.

Because I gave advice on marketing communications, I thought I had learned all there was to know about retailing. Nobody could have convinced me during the process that this project would fail. There was no way I could believe what I had learned while achieving my writing success would fail to transfer to a related enterprise.

The result was my spending hundreds of hours trying to convince the big bookstore chain they'd made a promise and not kept it. An entire spring and summer running season was missed as a result. And selling the maps was set back by a year. The designer/printer's bill sat on my desk and there were no sales coming in to offset the expense.

After three years the project still hadn't broken even. And though everybody who sees the map loves it, you can't take appreciation to the bank.

How can you profit from this experience?

Avoid these temptations and stick with the basics. Search out the businesses that need your writing skills. And avoid anything that seems like it's going to be an easy way to make extra money.

Stick to selling the best writing you can.

No Direct Access to the Client

Sometimes others will try to broker your services. This broker might be an advertising agency who doesn't have enough writers on staff. They will send an account executive to the client to get all the information. Then the A.E. meets with you to review the material and sends you off to write copy.

By the time you've gotten the information, it has been interpreted by the account executive. Then you've given it your creative treatment and go over that with the account executive again, who reinterprets it another time. Finally the client gets it without your being there, and what's been written may, by now, bear little resemblance to what they wanted in the first place.

Often this arrangement fails, and the writer gets blamed for that failure.

This happened to me in a way that seems laughable now. A small audio-visual production firm hired me to write scripts for them. The only employees were the director and a technical person. One of their wives came in to answer the phone and do the books a couple of times a week. It was a small operation.

Now people have every right to run their businesses the way they want, and this team wanted to be a small personalized company. They weren't overly ambitious and, frankly, it was my opinion that they thought too small. They weren't able to see the overall ways things worked in the business world.

185

The A.V. firm's owner/director made it a habit to meet with the client on his own to get the information about the projects. Then he'd schedule a meeting with the writer— me— and explain the information.

As the freelance writer, I would do my best to ask him questions at these meetings, but he wouldn't always have all the answers. He couldn't, since he thought about the problems of production rather than the content of the material, which is the writer's job.

At one juncture, there were two short video tapes to be done. They seemed straightforward enough from the second hand explanation I was given. One was a sales presentation and the other a video tape for a major trade show display booth in Europe. As usual these were rush-rush projects, so I stayed up all night doing them.

The next day, my A.V. producer and the client met to review the scripts. I was invited to the meeting for the first time. The first script was all right. But when we got to the second script, the client looked at it and said, "I think there's been some miscommunication here. You don't understand. This is for a trade show with an international, multilingual audience. It was to be visuals only. You weren't supposed to write any narration."

"Oh, I don't know how I missed that," said the audiovisual producer who hadn't let me meet with the client.

I cringed, thinking that if he was capable of missing a major point such as the fact that a presentation wasn't to have any narration, he must be skipping over an awful lot of more subtle bits of information along the way. Heavens knows what else he was forgetting to tell me.

Considering the circumstances, I did pretty well. I stepped in and explained that the basic concept of the show could be saved, and it would work as a silent piece. Because there was a solid structure to the program, the visuals could carry it along with a strong musical theme.

The client accepted this reasoning.

Later, the A.V. producer thanked me for saving him after he'd made this gross mistake. I never missed another client meeting after that.

Fight the efforts of people to keep you away from the clients you need to talk to for information. The farther you are away from the original information, the more likely you are to be blamed for mistakes that happen because of poor communication.

Just figure that if the people you work with aren't willing to take you along to meet the people paying the bills, they aren't too proud of you. Or they're hiding your existence. Or they probably aren't comfortable with their own relationship with the client. Don't allow yourself to be kept at a distance. It doesn't do anybody any good.

Get to the information source.

Impossible Assignment

Assuming you've tried your best, when clients decide your concept or your writing style won't work on a project, it won't. Nothing's going to get them to change their minds or look at your writing with an open mind if they've made the decision that it won't work.

This judgment can be presented harshly. It may be stated very matter-of-factly or it might be brought to your attention in a roundabout way. In any case, don't try to convince people they should like something you've written when they're determined not to.

If a client is unreasonable, maybe even childlike in their criticism, politely suggest it'd be best if they did the writing themselves.

"After all, you're the expert and it probably isn't possible for anyone except you to fully put forward the information in written form." This can be an appropriate response to a client who is harshly critical of your work and who thwarts your attempts to rewrite something.

Sometimes the reality of the client's having to write something on their own is so startling to them that they immediately approve what you've written. Other times they'll huff and puff, then finally come to terms with their own inadequacies and give you coherent directions.

Whatever happens, you want to be happy with your job. You want to enjoy writing and the contact with the client. If you don't have that, either change the relationship so that you are comfortable or find another client.

The Loneliness of the Freelance Business Writer

One of the downers about freelance writing is that you have to be by yourself for extended periods of time. Few people appreciate the number of hours spent alone hacking away at the keys, getting material out.

The only way to deal with the isolation is to decide you're going to enjoy it. The time you spend alone can be turned into a very positive experience.

Sometimes I'll have an assignment that stretches out over days. For practically the entire time, I'll go without seeing another human being. When this happens, it's easy to fall into the rhythm of your house. You know when the mail carrier will arrive. A chance phone call can change your attitude about life for hours. The refrigerator and telephone scream at you for attention. Ignored household tasks demand immediate completion.

You can fight the routine and solitary confinement in several ways. Making lunch dates is one of my favorites. This lets me work from about 8:30 until noon. Lunch lasts an hour or so, letting the batteries charge, then I'm back in the office working again by 2:00.

It's also constructive to set aside time for uninterrupted work. Two hours first thing in the morning is a good time. Let the answering machine field the calls, and return them when the two hours are up.

Client Cliques

Writing is a tough profession to pursue. Freelance writing for business is the easiest and most steady paying way to earn a living at writing today.

Writing, like any business, has traps. We fall into them and create them for ourselves in our own ways. We each have our own vulnerabilities. Things that don't phase one person devastate another.

Here are a few things to watch out for. These traps have set back business writers from the very first. You'll see them everyday as you do your work.

A trap which is very tough to overcome is the clique. These are groups of people with similar ideas and ways of looking at things who tend to stick together in organizations. They reinforce their own thinking and don't let other ideas in. These are sometimes called "opinion packs."

Business is full of them. Every corporation you work for will have these groups. They can work for you and against you. It's your job to stay clear of the opinion packs within your client's company. Your job as a writer is to be the outside influence that brings in fresh ideas. When you get into a group of people who constantly try the same approach to the same set of problems, your usefulness is lessened, and eventually the client's need for you evaporates.

Constantly broaden the scope of your interests and learn from many different types of people. To keep your perspective, spend time with people who aren't in the freelance writing business. My best breaks out of the business group are with people not remotely involved in marketing, advertising, or any aspect of corporate communications. One friend canoes and sells scales for a living, and another is a successful lawyer who looks at my freelance writing career with amusement. Another is a plumber.

It's all part of keeping your balance.

And the major balance for many of you will be how to apportion your time and interest between business writing and writing that novel—or those poems—or those short stories.

Chapter 13

Keeping Your Work Positive

A Matter of Attitude

Believe that you can make it as a freelance writer. Have a positive self-image and believe in your writing ability. Believe that you and your work have real value.

Sound like excerpts from a salesmanship course? Or like verbiage from a Sunday morning pop-religion TV program? Or some sort of contemporary psychology drivel?

It may be all these things.

However, it is true. Sum it up to say that your attitude has everything to do with your potential for success as a freelance writer.

In personal growth terms, we call this a positive mental attitude. Or stated as a sports metaphor, "putting down your head and running with the ball". In religion it might be "keeping the faith." Whichever way it manifests itself, believing in yourself will make the difference in whether you succeed at writing or give it up to go back to something else.

What does this mean in practical terms? Don't waste your time on petty matters. Get down to business and get your work done. Always smile. Telling you to smile and be nice sounds simplistic and obvious. But so many would-be freelancers don't work at being pleasant, easy to get along with, and just plain friendly.

You want people to be delighted to see you.

I worked with a freelance graphic artist on and off for a couple of years. His work was good. His fees were fair or maybe a little high at times. Unfortunately there was a tendency on the artist's part to be mad at the world. He wasn't mad at it once in a while. He was steamed under the surface nearly every time I saw him.

At a client meeting, he would often sit silently, almost brooding. He gave the impression he was upset about something and, if asked, there would often be some small matter that was irking him. A couple of times he had used inappropriate language and offended clients the first time he'd met them.

Basically, the guy had an attitude problem. It may have come from his hours of isolated work. It might have been the result of family problems or trouble in a relationship.

Whatever it was, more than one client expressed concern, not over the quality of the work, but over the artist's attitude. After all, who wants to work with someone who is unhappy every time you see him? Nobody wants to be locked in a month-long project with a person who can't display a positive attitude throughout—particularly in the writing business, which is full of its own problems.

The message is: relax and enjoy your work. Ideas come easier when you're relaxed. Problems can be worked out when you're comfortable with yourself. You have a lot more energy to work with when you're easy about things and when you strive to make others feel comfortable with you.

If writing isn't fun, it's not worth the trouble—whether you're getting paid or not.

Sure there are lousy clients. Some days you will wonder how a company as big and profitable as the one you're working for could hire such buffoons to work for it.

Walk up the steps to your front door, after a day of trying to work with a corporation, and say to yourself, "I'm a writer, independent of these people. I have my own writing to do. There are things that interest me that I can write about with a great deal of understanding. I am able to express myself well and my talent is able to overcome any petty crisis these guys are going to toss in front of me."

Knowing that you aren't trapped in the system is very liberating. The feeling of separation and independence you have when you freelance can work for you when you're down.

Let's Be Realistic: It Can Be Bad

To make it, you have to have stamina. Your belief in yourself has to be strong. It can be bad out there. There are days when you want to hang it all up and go into the dry cleaning business, or some other equally honorable and predictable profession.

I've had days when I was ready to quit the whole thing, live in a burrow in a rural part of a prairie state and write trashy novels. It seems noble to starve when you're writing. The image of a struggling writer is very romantic. Many writers insist on living it. It's a very comfortable and familiar vision. But a drag to actually live through.

One incident sticks in my mind. It was minor, but was part of a build-up that any freelancer will want to watch out for.

There was a corporation with big budgets selling financial services. They had the potential to become a major client if I could get in and play things right.

I made the proper phone calls to find out who the decision-maker was—the individual who hired freelance writers.

When I make these cold calls, I'll usually ask, if I don't have a name to begin with, "Who hires freelance writers on your staff?" or "Who manages the writing services in your department?"

This got me connected with a man who had worked in the same section of the company for a long, long time. When I met him, he spent all our time telling me about his career. My experience has been that in an interview situation like this, people who spend all the time talking about themselves have not worked through some major personal problems. They probably feel stuck in their jobs, and they believe that others in their company are watching and waiting for them to retire.

I did what I was supposed to do with this man. I asked him about work, but couldn't get him off himself. He went on about his career as if it were already over, to the extent of telling me which bus he took into the office everyday and how he timed the transfers.

When I was finally able to ask him about the opportunities available for freelance writing in the company, there seemed to be many. Volumes of printed materials were generated by this corporation and distributed to sales reps and customers all across the country. They produced tons of information, all needing writers.

I phoned periodically to check in with him.

A year later I bumped into the man at a design firm's open house inaugurating a new office. I reintroduced myself and asked if it was worth my staying in touch for work.

You can feel very self-conscious about coming right out and asking for work like this, especially at a social gathering. But what's the point of hinting around? If the person's going to give you an assignment, it's probably because you were the last one who asked. If you never had a chance anyway, you have nothing to lose by asking. At worst, they'll tell you to go talk to another person in their organization.

In any case, I asked and he told me, "I tried to reach you once about six months ago. I let the phone ring many times and there was no answer. I couldn't get a hold of you, so the project went elsewhere."

I was ready to push the man down on the floor and strangle him. I'd been trying to break into that company for months, and he's telling me he tried but couldn't reach me. This was impossible to believe. My answering machine is on 24 hours a day. If it's not working, I'd know very quickly. And if he really wanted to reach me, he would have given it more than one shot.

I really believe he was lying.

The best way to handle this sort of situation is to be cordial. I sent him a note the next day with another business card so he could be sure to check his listing of my phone number.

I never did work for the man or the king-size company he worked for. It just wasn't in the cards at that time. When I think back on it, I wonder if he actually had any authority to give assignments at all. He didn't seem very busy and there was little in his office to indicate that he was doing any work.

Here's another unproven fact: people with nothing on their desk and without anything cluttering up their offices don't really have much to do. They either haven't been given any responsibility, or they haven't taken it.

This man had a very clean desk.

195

Clean desk or not, the rule is not to waste your time with people who can't help you succeed.

Don't Complain—Change

It is always easier to complain about a situation and let it go than to do something about it. And whatever happens to you, it's always a greater challenge to remember the good things than the bad. Something about human nature makes us dwell on misfortune.

Being assertive in finding clients or handling frustrating situations as they come up doesn't mean you have to be mad at anybody. It doesn't mean you have to come at problems in an abrasive manner or try to punish people.

Being a little irreverent about your approach to business means using your intuition in finding work, developing ways to select the clients you want, and not being intimidated by corporations, whether they're huge mega-organizations or small family-run shops.

Success at freelance writing means tossing away the misconceptions you have about helpless writers and freelancing in particular. It means not making things hard on yourself because you're afraid to tell a client what you really think about something.

Remember that you can't please everybody. Don't hesitate dropping clients you don't work well with. Let clients go if you don't get a feeling of satisfaction from working with them. Enjoy your work and eliminate things from your freelance business writing activity that don't suit you. Make it easy and happy for yourself.

Form a Writers' Group

Another positive activity to end writer's isolation is to form a group of freelancers who get together once a month or so. I meet every four to six weeks with 15 to 40 freelance communicators.

These aren't only people doing freelance business writing. They are a group of people who handle communications for newspapers, magazines, public relations, software documentation, and many other activities. There may be tech writers, housewives and husbands who work very little, full-time writers, artists, and a variety of others making moderate to good incomes.

The criteria we have established for membership in the writers group is at least some professional experience. Writers have to have been writing at least a full year and it must be their principal source of income. This is difficult to enforce, and the rules have been bent to let some people in.

Organizing the meetings is generally the responsibility of a volunteer. We meet at a restaurant that doesn't mind having a group take up a back room.

We have shared information about deadbeats. We've brought in an accountant, a lawyer, a Small Business Administration official, and other professionals to give us advice. It's also an informal support group, since we share how we're handling our common concerns. Meeting once a month is just often enough.

Take Vacations

Block out one- or two-week slots for time off and protect the free time you've scheduled. I'll guarantee that whatever time you pick to leave town on a vacation, a big assignment will come up. This has happened to me consistently over the years. I'll be packing a suitcase for a Christmas trip to visit the family and the phone will ring. Sure enough, it's a video producer I haven't heard from in years, wanting me to write a major assignment overnight.

Go ahead and go on vacation. Forget the assignment. You need some diversion, too. The worst thing you can do is get so wrapped up in your work that you can't ever get away from it.

Keep Your Perspective

It is easy to get discouraged. Especially when you're tired from too much work on a subject you don't like, you'll wonder if writing is what you really want to do for a living. The solution is to find ways to get perspective on your writing. I find that by visiting a person with a corporate job at their office, I'm convinced very quickly that I don't want that routine.

Persistence Pays

Talent alone isn't enough to make it as a freelance writer. I wish it were. Much better writers than you or I are selling plumbing parts and driving buses. Very good and smart writers have taken an excursion into freelancing for a while and then left it. There is nothing wrong with them, and they had every right to get in and eventually give up.

The biggest thing that separates success from failure is persistence. Just plain sticking to it. Writing is not easy. Lots of bad things will happen. Plenty of things will go wrong. Typewriters will break in the middle of major assignments—on holiday weekends when they can't be fixed. Favorite clients will be fired or move out of town just as you've cultivated them. People will try to involve you in corporate politics. You'll do everything you can to keep clear of it, but somehow you will become involved.

Success and failure will come at the same time—and occasionally it's difficult to tell the difference.

Persistence is the deciding factor. If you stick with it, you will make it. There is no other guarantee any one can offer you. There is a market for your skills. Somehow you will be able to make the connections to get into the cash flow. It will take time and it won't be easy. Once you've decided you want to be a writer, this is the way to earn a living at it. Get into freelancing for business. From this you will also learn the techniques of managing freelance writing of all types.

Chapter 14

Growing As You Write

Visualizing Success

Freelance writing for business is not selling out. The same writing skills work for business that work for any other type of writing.

There are differences between business communications and what you've been writing before. Certain peculiarities take getting use to, but once you learn about them, you can handle any kind of writing assignment that comes your way. You will be able to earn a living at it if you want.

Unfortunately, what you want to get from writing and what the profession has, realistically, to offer are probably different things. Read the biography of any author to discover that struggle. It's tough, not only to be so self-motivated that you sit down and write without someone looking over your shoulder, but to keep your head together while facing practical matters like mortgage payments and trips to the supermarket.

Sometime when you are in a reflective frame of mind, sit down on the floor with your back against the wall. Close your eyes and take some deep breaths. After a couple of minutes of grounding yourself this way, begin to imagine yourself in an office. It's a perfect writing office that you designed and built exactly to your specifications.

All the books you need to do your research are there. A telephone is within arm's reach. Dialing it gives you access to the smartest research librarians in the world. At your desk is just the type of word processor you like. The keyboard has the perfect touch and your comfortable chair raises you to the exact height to make typing a breeze.

The setup couldn't be better. The wall color always puts you in the mood to write. The carpet is lush, its design and feel are soothing. In fact, there is nothing of the outside world to take your attention away from the writing you want to do.

Let this image of the perfect work space come alive. Imagine yourself in it, sitting at the desk. See yourself getting up to check a reference book on the big set of shelves. You go back to the keyboard and continue working on your writing project.

Now answer these questions. Where is this office? What kind of word processing system are you working on in it? Is it an old typewriter or a computer-driven machine? What sort of carpet is it and what books are on the shelves that you are using to do your work?

Keep these answers in mind. They represent your ideal writing setup. Stay seated against the wall and keep that living image of your perfect office in mind.

Now let's stir in the practical part of your mind. This is the part of your consciousness that opens the bills that come in the mail. It writes the checks to pay those bills. This part of your mind balances your check book and makes sure all the numbers add up.

The most important question is: what were you writing to be able to afford the perfect office?

Wait! Don't answer—don't answer. Breath deeply.

Breathe once more.

Imagine you're supporting yourself by writing for corporations. Your continuing clients are businesses. They are calling you on a regular basis with assignments. On your desk is the morning mail.

See yourself opening it. It is full of letters from these companies. Several letters have congratulations and thanks for your writing. Copies of your printed articles, press releases, and brochures spill out of larger envelopes. They've sent you a video tape cassette, too. It's a program you wrote the script for, so you play it. The show is great, and you enjoy seeing your ideas come to life.

In the rest of the mail are checks from these companies. Each is paying an invoice you sent in recently. You're glad your clients pay so quickly.

You notice the time. Better get back to your current project, since you've got a deadline to meet in a couple of days. You spent the morning working on your novel and budgeted the afternoon for your business clients.

Your day is your own. The business clients are a pleasure to work with. There is positive energy from every one of them. You enjoy trips to their offices. Dressing up in their style of business clothes amuses you. It's a nice change from the jeans and T-shirt you often choose to wear at home.

Gradually let yourself come out of this daydream. Feel your back against the wall and your feet on the floor.

Open your eyes and look around the room. Now think over what you've imagined. Consider the opportunities business writing will offer you. How will it help you do more writing? Does the idea of deadlines seem a little less scary? Wouldn't you like to have "articles" assigned and sold before you write them? Isn't it nice to have the people who will edit your writing in town and available to meet with you, rather than carrying on long distance correspondence and phone contact with editors of periodicals?

The biggest problem I've seen with people wanting to get into business writing is fear of not understanding what it's all about. They don't realize the potential for producing income from their writing. Often I've also sensed a fear of giving up something in their writing that they'll never get back when they write for corporations.

They could not be further from the truth. Unlike the writing a lawyer or a reporter does, which encourages conformity to specific standards, business writing encourages you to develop your own style, but to adapt it to meet others' needs. The more you write, the better you get.

What makes your business writing better is the same stuff that improves your short stories and helps novels come alive. And because you become familiar with the give and take of editors and practice writing constantly, doors are opened to magazine markets. Plus—you are provided with the machinery and resources to do any other writing that interests you. You can let business writing "support your habit"—of writing poetry, screenplays, novels or whatever. You can decide where to focus your future writing efforts.

Is That All There Is To It?

Being a writer is one of the best professions anyone can have. You can define what you are as a writer any way you want, to whomever you want. The worst and the best thing about the title "writer" is that it's available to anyone who wants it.

People call themselves writers who have barely written more than their names on driver's licenses. You can hardly go to any gathering without someone proclaiming to be a writer, even though you suspect they haven't cranked a sheet of paper through a typewriter in years.

On the positive side, you don't need a string of degrees to become a writer. And the fact that you can announce that you are one at any time and take up the profession full-blast at a moment's notice has a certain accessible charm about it.

Freelance writing only requires that you have common sense. Your success relies primarily on this common sense and persistence, rather than on any inherent intellect. These are the greatest assets you can bring to it. Common sense is the ingredient missing from many business decisions and the cause of most of the blunders people in companies make. Lack of persistence is why many try freelancing and give up.

Your ability to combine your desire to be a writer, your organizational skills, common sense, persistence, and perspective from the outside of a business can make you its champion—and provide you with an income available in few other writing fields.

have to tell you this, rather than simply find self-satisfaction in knowing it about themselves, and letting their knowledge and craftsmanship in writing flower quietly during the rewriting process. Clearly they have some insecurities brewing that can bubble up and burn you later.

Listen for individuals who declare something on the order of, "I consider myself a good writer. I have a B.A. and a Masters Degree in journalism. I've been trained in the writing craft. I lived and breathed writing for six years in college."

If you hear this, and these quotes are practically verbatim from an experience of mine, try to get up and run.

An example of this was when I was called in by a major bank to write articles for their in-house publication. It was basically a small newsletter, distributed to employees every week. The initial two minutes of the meeting with the editor went well enough. Unfortunately it was a ten-minute meeting.

At first there were the standard hellos, exchange of business cards and formalities. Then, out of the blue, the lady began talking about her little newsletter as if it were the Sunday *New York Times*. She positioned herself as the editor of this flagship of periodicals, the editorial thrust of which took its readers on a voyage to the deepest understanding of the human soul, not merely through the portals of employee retirement updates, bowling league scores, and corporate trivia.

Needless to say, she preceded to give me her credentials. Her undergraduate and graduate degrees were in journalism. Consequently, she reasoned, everyone like her who worked on newsletters like hers were "professional journalists."

Just between you and me, she worked for a bank. Period! Now it's a big bank, so big it needs this little newsletter to give everyone a sense of community. She may consider herself a journalist, and there's nothing wrong with that. But based on past experience, and judging from the tone of her conversation, I begged off from the assignments she was offering. My excuse was that the time frame was too short and that scheduling problems wouldn't allow me to do the job right. I knew that neither she nor I would ever feel satisfied with what either one of us wrote, said, or did.

Freelance business writing success is based largely on the chemistry between you and your client. Always look for friendly people with a good perspective on things. They're out there, even though it may feel like it takes a lot of looking to find them.

We'll Give You One More Try

Odd circumstances abound in freelance business writing. You will have a wide variety of experiences. You'll be able to travel to strange places: from a fire-breathing, smoke-belching factory to the rarified atmosphere of an executive board room where everybody makes over a million bucks a year.

Clients will fly you around in corporate jets. You will get to stay in every sort of accommodation from the worst flea-bag motels to super-nice, first-rate establishments. It can be great, if you're willing to put up with the down times and all the bends and curves along the road.

Strange occurrences may happen at any time. Imagine yourself in this one.

A very large audio-visual production firm was known to be very tough for a freelancer to crack. The one man who was supposed to be the contact for freelance writers was highly impersonal. He'd act as if you had awakened him in

172

the middle of the night when calling him on the phone at work to introduce yourself. He was abrupt, cutting off conversations, and just basically rude. I tried calling the firm's president, but the calls were never returned.

I had been working on a potential client at a major corporation for some time. This person had reign over large budgets and periodically hired the audio-visual firm that I'd been trying to crack. At a lunch meeting with the potential client, we ran into the president of the A.V. firm and I was introduced to him. I greeted him and went on to say that I'd tried to get him on the phone five times in the last two months to show him my work.

Of course, in the presence of one of his clients, he melted a little, telling me to call that afternoon for an appointment.

I did and ended up showing my portfolio and talking with him for an hour. The next thing I knew, something was said to someone else, and this man who was previously so curt called me with three assignments. Being introduced to the president of the A.V. firm got me started. It looked like I could become one of their favored writers.

Immediately everything went awful. The man who had been so rude continued that way. I didn't have the opportunity to write a first draft on a single script. In fact, I did one outline of an assignment (using their formula) and got a call.

"I'm taking you off these assignments."

"What's the matter?" I couldn't believe what I was hearing.

"It's the writing," he said. "It just isn't any good."

"But, I haven't even been able to do any writing yet."

And I hadn't. The only thing I'd been able to write for them was their tired old formula outline for the show that puffed up their concern for the client without stating any particular approach to the material.

The real problem was that there wasn't any one person in the A.V. firm I was to report to. Everybody in the organization was afraid to take responsibility for the material, and everyone was so loaded with work they were tired all the time. Nothing was getting accomplished. It turned out that the big successful audio-visual firm was an organizational nightmare, barely staying ahead of its deadlines.

The big mistake I made with them was to write a rough draft of one of the scripts, label it "First Draft" and leave it for one of their staff to review. I wanted to get a reaction to the material as I understood it because all the people on the project were headed in so many directions that there was no focus.

I complained to the president about the treatment I received, and they decided they'd give me "one more chance" to get the first draft right.

At the time I was learning the ropes and figured this situation was common. Let me tell you it is not at all common and I was very much taken advantage of because I wanted to please them. Doing this, I sacrificed what my own instincts were telling me.

I attended another meeting and got even more information for a rewrite. Then I stayed up all night and wrote what I thought was a fine first draft. I turned it in and got another phone call.

"No, I'm sorry. This just doesn't make it. That's it, you're done."

I was taken off the project because they said they didn't like the second draft either.